Dr Michael Sharon is a leading worldwide expert on nutrition and is the author of bestselling nutrition titles including *Complete Nutrition, Eat to Live* and *Nutrients A–Z*. A pioneer in the field of natural nutrition for almost three decades, Dr Sharon has been researching and expounding on healthy eating habits in his busy nutrition practice as well as being a popular public speaker and a magazine writer. When a series of intense personal crises in his younger years plunged him into an abyss of deep despondency, Dr Sharon embarked on a spiritual quest in an attempt to find meaning for his life's trials. During many years of soul searching, Dr Sharon came to realize the crucial value of self-love as a basic tool for spiritual evolution and started to share his insights with his patients. As word of mouth spread, people were increasingly seeking him more as a spiritual guide rather than a nutritional consultant. He now shares his ideas in this book to help people see the beneficial lessons of their own predicaments and rise to higher levels of love, peace and happiness.

THE MAGIC OF SELF-ACCEPTANCE

How to be Happy

Dr Michael Sharon

Book Guild Publishing

Sussex, England

First published in Great Britain in 2008 by
The Book Guild Ltd
Pavilion View
19 New Road
Brighton, BN1 1UF

Typesetting in Times by
SetSystems Ltd, Saffron Walden, Essex

Printed in Great Britain by
Athenaeum Press Ltd, Gateshead

A catalogue record for this book is
available from the British Library

ISBN 978 1 84624 209 0

To Christina
my soulmate

Contents

You must love yourself
Before you love another.

By accepting yourself
And joyfully being
What you are,
You fulfil your own abilities
And your simple presence
Can make
Others happy.

Jane Roberts
The Nature of Personal Reality

Preface

'You are what you eat, drink and think' is the first sentence of my book, *Complete Nutrition*. A decade after the first edition of this classic work has been published, I feel it is time to share with my readers the lessons I have learned in the school of life, along my own growth path. Although as a nutritionist I have been educated to believe that the scourges of humanity can be solved by natural foods and supplements, I now feel that the end of the first sentence, the 'think', may be even more important. And that is because I came to realise that it is our mental diet that eventually determines our life's experiences.

I decided to write this book after many years of trudging along the path of evolution, trying to make sense of everything that has been happening in my life. It is strange how sometimes things happen. Some thirty years ago, I bought a book for my cousin, who at that time was going through a personal crisis. He showed little interest in having it and I ended up reading it myself. This book was to put me on my growth path and eventually, became my companion for a number of years while I was trying to assimilate its values. The title of the book, by the late Dr Norman Vincent Peale, was *The Power of Positive Thinking*. Other books followed in perfect timing, each taking me up to the next level, as if an unseen hand was guiding me perfectly on my spiritual quest. It was a classical example of the aphorism, 'When the student is ready, the teacher appears.' Only in this case, my teacher was not human but, rather, was divine guidance.

In my scientific training I was taught to think rationally, in accepted frames and structures, and trust only in what can be proven according to preset research protocols, such as double-blind studies. I was trained to have a 'scientific tunnel vision'. Anecdotal evidence was totally unacceptable even if it felt right within. I did not trust my inner voice and my impulses. No wonder that when I graduated, I came to ignore my feelings and consider only my rationale as the ultimate wisdom. I did not trust my intuition enough to act on its messages, since they often made no sense to my intellect and anyway, I did not have the courage to act on them. Logic felt safer. In other words, I did not trust my divine part. And each time I ignored my inner urges I eventually lived to regret having done so.

As a child, I was led to believe that other people were more important. That other people came first. For many years I did not know what self-love really meant. I would confuse it with egoism. I did not think I was important enough and did not have much self-confidence. How could I, when I was validating and supporting other people before me at my expense? I simply did not know to draw a line, to assert myself. No wonder that I was making unwise decisions in my personal life and paying the highest price in misery and unhappiness. It took me many years to grasp the fundamental concept of self-love. Indeed, self-love became the starting point in my own evolution. I finally realised that in order to make my life work, to grow, to succeed, to achieve happiness and to be of service to my fellow humans, I must first learn to practise more self-love.

In broad terms, our consciousness is composed of two parts, which are commonly referred to as 'higher consciousness' and 'lower consciousness'. Or in simpler words, one part is self-love and one part is self-hate, the latter being the part of the ego. These parts oppose one another. They each have contrasting attributes which we can all find within us. Spiritual growth is about using self-love to heal our consciousness from self-hate aberrations. It means that just by increasing self-love we transform our non-loving flaws into loving virtues. We can thus help upgrade our fear to faith. As the part of self-love in our consciousness is increased, the part of self-hate is automatically decreased.

The following illustration lists some main attributes of our consciousness. Can you spot the ones you act more frequently? Do you know which unloving roles you would like to tone down? Do you know which loving ones you want to promote?

CONSCIOUSNESS

HIGHER	*LOWER*
SELF-LOVE	SELF-HATE
Faith	Fear
Truth	Lies
Constructiveness	Destructiveness
Self-assertion	Self-deprecation
Self-reward	Self-punishment
Will to succeed	Will to fail
Prosperity awareness	Scarcity concerns
Salubrious practices	Harmful addictions
Healthy diet; exercise; meditation	Smoking; drinking; drugs
Health	Disease
Humility and compassion	Conceit and aggression

Acceptance	Criticism
Happiness	Unhappiness
Modesty	Ego trips

Increase self-love to reduce self-hate

During my years on the path, I gradually learned this great truth. I have come to realise that in order to eliminate the darkness of lower consciousness, you don't have to resist it, fight it or stamp over it. All you need to do is to shed light on it. Just shine it away with the light of love. On the journey to enlightenment, you can similarly expand your consciousness just by becoming more aware of your inherent love. As Carl Jung once said, 'One does not become enlightened by imagining figures of light but by making the darkness conscious.'

By increasing my own self-love I started to reconnect with my divine love, the great love inside each of us which is part of the Universal Mind. I gradually started to actually feel that the 'kingdom of God is within me'. That I am taken care of on a higher level by a divine power that loves me. I have learned that ultimately, everything happens for a good reason and that each painful experience, misfortune or crisis, is in fact a learning opportunity and each has a beneficial message. A message that is intended to lead us all to higher states of consciousness.

Eventually, I began to change my concepts. I did not feel alone any more. I could increasingly sense a divine plan perfectly unfolding in my life, leading me to ascend and transcend, raising me gradually to higher levels of consciousness, giving me a sense of direction and purpose, and often, making way for me where I could see no way. I started to notice miraculous occurrences in my life that defied explanation. In time, I found the courage to take the leap of faith and surrender to the higher power; let God run my life. I finally realised that the sufferings I endured for so many years were caused by my ego's resistance to the flow of life; by my resistance to heed the call of grace. I could finally identify with the words of the famous hymn, 'Amazing Grace', 'I once was lost but now I'm found, was blind but now I see.'

My own growth was to be reflected in my practice as nutritional consultant. I began to notice that after a consultation, a patient would remain sitting, looking at me as if expecting something extra, beyond nutritional advice, something spiritual. When I would suggest a change in mental attitudes and a different outlook, the patient's face would light up and they would listen intently to what I had to suggest. It was amazing to note how patients were using fearful and self-defeating thoughts to create disease; how many did not realise that their insecurity and feeling of unworthiness were promoting various afflictions from recurrent colds to hypertension and from exhaustion to heart disease. More than nutritional deficiencies, these people were demonstrating a deficiency in self-love.

I feel that it is now time to share what I have learned so far in my own journey. To expound the idea that life is simple, and that it is us who make it complicated by resisting its natural flow. That although pain is an inevitable part of life, self-torment is optional. Yet on the other hand, it is not mandatory to grow through pain; we can simply choose to grow with joy. We live in a world of various illusionary emotions where only love is real. I came to realise that love is the path to joy; that happiness is an inner choice that does not have to depend on outer experiences. And that, in the words of the Dalai Lama, 'The purpose of life is to seek happiness.'

Writing this book has been an adventure which I was led into. Even the idea to write it came up unexpectedly, following a chance remark made by the former publisher of my nutritional books. In the beginning, I had only a notion of the title and some vague concepts for the first chapter. The rest was a mystery. But I guess the higher Will must have wanted this book because I was gradually sent flashes of inspiration and subtle insights, along with wonderful friends who gave me the encouraging feedback that I needed to strengthen my resolve.

I like to extend heartfelt gratitude to my spiritual path companion Gail Lazar, who went over the first draft and provided many enlightening comments, to my friends Mozelle Elias and Dennis Clark for their constructive feedback, to my devoted editors Joanna Bentley and Mandy Woods, who polished the text and last but not least, to my publisher Carol Biss, whose enthusiastic support made this book a reality. May they all be blessed.

1

Self-Love versus Egoism

A book about self-love? Is this a manual promoting conceited selfishness? Aren't we supposed to forget ourselves and think of others as we aspire to promote higher moral values and spiritual growth? No. At least not in that order. In Buddhism, self-love comes first. Before all else, Buddhists strive for personal perfection, from which right thoughts and right actions arise. They call it Mettā (a sublime form of loving kindness). They would say mentally, 'May I be well and happy,' and then, after a while, they will extend it to all others by saying, 'May all beings of the universe be well and happy.' If a person cannot love himself, they reckon, how can he love others? A modern analogy can be heard in the safety instructions during any airline flight. In case of emergency, when oxygen masks are automatically dropped, parents are instructed to first put on their own masks, before putting them on their children.

The Bible itself refers to self-love when it commands, 'Love thy neighbour as thyself.' But what if you do not love yourself? How will you then be able to love your neighbour? Self-love comes before universal love. Self-love is the cornerstone, the foundation of our emotional system. It is a prerequisite in any quest for spiritual evolution. The development of self-love was once compared to pouring wine into a glass, when the wine symbolises love and the glass represents our mind. Not until the glass is filled to its rim

1

will the wine start running over. All love starts with self-love.

Egoism, on the other hand, has nothing to do with love. It is uncontrolled narcissism, an overcompensation for the lack of self-love. The most important thing for ego-driven people is not self-love; it is self-esteem and self-pride. What they care most about is the external image that they project to the outside world; the respect, reverence and honour that they can command.

Egoism is a fearful concept of survival. When we identify with it, it disconnects us from our higher loving self. The universe operates naturally in a system of infinite love and compassion, prosperity and abundance. The fear of the ego is based on false concepts of scarcity and insecurity. The ego keeps its grip by making us feel needy and powerless. It creates an insatiable hunger to snatch everything in sight—money, power, sex and pleasure. These are supposed to fill an imaginary lack, but they never do. An inner emptiness can only be filled from within by growth of consciousness, never from an outer supply. To develop self-love, we constantly have to keep cutting back our narcissism and our self-centredness. We need to eradicate our false pride. This is not an easy task. Nor is it done in a single attempt. It is a lifetime endeavour.

Egoism is about limitations. It perceives that 'there is not enough'. Scarcity perceptions lead to aggressiveness and wars. In fact, the fear of the ego is at the root of all evil in this world. It causes greed, jealousies, possessiveness, conflicts, unhappiness and disease. It leads egocentric people to blame and manipulate others.

And since it is the opposite of love and oneness, the ego is about hatred and separateness; separation from mankind. This is a violation of the sacred truth of the oneness of humanity, which was so exquisitely expressed in the following way by John Donne: 'No man is an island, entire of

2

itself; every man is a piece of the continent, a part of the maine.'

How can we simultaneously be both distinct individuals and part of the whole? Let us consider the metaphor of an ocean and waves, in which people are symbolised by waves while the vast ocean represents the collective human consciousness. Just as each wave has its own individual shape, intensity and life-span, so do we humans have each our individual traits, while still being part of the cosmic ocean. Just like waves, we perform individual roles during our lifetimes and then merge again with the spiritual ocean, the divine pool of universal consciousness from which we originated.

We finally realise that we are all made up of the same stuff and animated by the same energy. And the underlying power that keeps us unified is the universal life-sustaining love which knows no separateness. As we gradually develop a sense of unison with humanity, it is much easier to feel unconditional acceptance with everyone. After all, why should one drop of water despise the next drop? Aren't they all part of the same ocean which is the source of their existence? The concept of oneness, once realised, not only expands self-love but also develops within us a sense of brotherhood with humanity. Everyone is your brother or sister, friend and foe alike. We thus learn to accept people for who they are, not for who we would prefer them to be.

The ego is about vanity and conceit, while our higher self is about humility and compassion. In *Soul Prints*, spiritual teacher Marc Gafni makes the subtle distinction between the two: 'To be ego-driven is to think you are God. To be pulled by the soul print is to know you are God.' An egocentric person is actually godless; he is detached from his divine part; he feels he is on his own in this world; he believes he has no allies. This feeling of isolation is very daunting. To evolve, we must release our fears by starting

3

to realise that we are not lone beings but part of a divine wholeness. To promote self-love we must learn to accept ourselves with all our 'flaws'. We have to gradually free ourselves from the ties of the ego. As Albert Einstein said, 'The true value of a human being is determined primarily by the measure and the sense in which he has obtained liberation from the self [ego].'

By transcending the boundaries of the ego we can reach out to our soul, our divine part which knows no limits, no fear, no scarcity, no separateness. Distinguishing between the ego and the soul is a constant reminder of our divinity. As the nineteenth-century mystic Sri Ramakrishna explained, 'Know thyself, and you shall then know the non-self and the Lord of All. What is my ego? Is it my hand, or foot, or flesh, or blood, or muscle, or tendon? Ponder deep, and you shall know that there is no such thing as I. As by continually peeling off the skin of the onion, so by analysing the ego, it will be found that there is not any real entity corresponding to the ego. The ultimate result of all such analysis is God. When egoism drops away, Divinity manifests itself.'

Self-love is a primary moral duty from which all other virtues branch out. That is why it is so crucially important for growth. The more you practise self-love and self-acceptance, the more you align yourself with the loving power of all creation. This makes you more powerful. Self-love, however, is not a finite goal. It is a lifetime endeavour. It is a lifelong journey of spiritual quest, because no matter how high we evolve, there are always higher levels to reach.

Many people doubt the need to promote self-love. After all, they would argue, isn't it a natural instinct of survival? Self-love, however, goes much deeper than a mere survival instinct. It is an all-inclusive awareness with many aspects; you can love yourself in some ways but not in others. That is why people can be self-destructive in certain matters, while acting constructively in other situations. And that is why so many of us fail to evolve spiritually and achieve the health, success and happiness we all deserve.

Non-loving traits are usually formed during early childhood years through faulty educational concepts used even by well-meaning parents. Telling a child what to do is one thing, but telling a child what he is, or is not, can either boost or undermine the kid's self-image. Condemning remarks like 'You are lazy', 'You are not as good as your brother' or 'You are clumsy' impair the natural self-confidence and block the flow of self-love in specific areas; they can traumatise a child's consciousness, often for life. In fact, parents can instill insecurity and self-deprecating patterns in their children without even saying a word. Children are very sensitive. They can sense mental attitudes in parents and adopt them as modes of behaviour. That is why we need to expand our awareness of self-love in adulthood by reprogramming old concepts that we have outgrown. And as self-love expands, it spreads out into our unloving aspects and heals them.

Self-love may be likened to a large crystal with many facets, some of which are polished and shiny while others are unpolished and dim. You may, for example, love yourself enough to eat healthily but hate the clumsy way you act around people. To promote self-love we need to 'polish' our non-loving aspects by loving them, not by hating them. And as you send them love, they will have much less hold on you.

Self-love is unconditional self-acceptance. You accept the way you look, the way you act and the way you think. Self-love does not wait for the day when you will look better, feel happier or become more successful. Self-love is a conscious commitment to love yourself as you are *right now*. It is a commitment to honour your feelings and take responsibility for your own happiness. There are no exceptions to this decision. You pledge to appreciate, support and validate yourself at the present time, without judgement or criticism. And just like God, you are forgiving yourself all your iniquities and wrongdoings. It means stepping out of guilt for anything you may have done in the past; relieving yourself from the burden of past misconducts. Realising that the past has to be buried before a better future can evolve.

You are your own best friend. Anybody in your life may one day leave you. Even the most harmonious marriages end when 'death do us part'. But you will never leave. You are here for life. So treat yourself well, as you would treat a best friend. Be there for yourself. Be supportive, helpful and, especially, uncritical. Strive to love yourself as you actually are. And when you treat yourself well, you will find that the whole world treats you better. What goes around comes around.

In fact, you must learn to love and accept yourself *before* starting a romantic relationship. You must feel that your heart is already full of love, so that you do not even need somebody else's love to feel fulfilled. If you do not truly love yourself, if you do not feel lovable, how will you accept someone else's love for you? It will be impossible for the other person to communicate with you in loving ways. The most loving partner cannot make you feel beloved if you do not deem yourself lovable.

Self-love is the foundation for spiritual growth. It is the springboard that propels us in our journey to higher consciousness and personal evolution. It is the path to health, happiness and prosperity. When we aspire to grow and evolve, self-love is a prerequisite. And as we learn to love ourselves more, we find that all aspects of self-love are identical to those of universal love. In our quest for self-love we develop virtues that are extended to our spiritual growth and make our journey much easier.

6

Why wouldn't anyone be self-loving? Why are so many of us afflicted with self-resentment, tormented by insecurity and ravaged by self-abuse? The answer is that we have forgotten our natural identity of divine love and, instead, opted to reside in the ego and adopt its fears and insecurities. It is easy to identify with the ego. The ego works logically, in a linear dimension, in a way our intellect can understand. The ego says that the end justifies the means; it gives us a free hand to act immorally. It allows us to ignore our values and do whatever it takes in order to achieve. It pushes us to struggle, bully, manipulate, bend rules, commit crimes and compromise our integrity. And 'once you get rid of integrity, the rest is a piece of cake'. This phrase, uttered by JR Ewing in the TV series *Dallas*, illustrates how the ego works. You give it a finger and it takes the whole hand. But struggle is the opposite of surrender.

When we struggle to manipulate events beyond our control, we resist. When we surrender, we flow freely with the stream of life. It is usually after a long phase of grappling with adversity, when we get so fed up struggling and striving, that we finally muster the courage to take the leap of faith and surrender. And when we let go and flow with loving acceptance of the here and now, divine power takes over. This is when great things can happen. So act responsibly, give up control!

Imagine a paratrooper who is about to jump from the safety of a plane into the thin air and has to overcome a paralysing fear of the unknown. It seems like leaping into a daunting emptiness. He could not jump unless he trusts the parachute to sustain him in this void. Likewise, we have to surrender to the flow of life. Our parachute is our faith. When we jump into the uncertainty of life—that is, when, like the paratrooper, we take the leap of faith—we discover that we are sustained by an invisible power, a higher power that loves us and takes care of us if only we let it, if only we

7

surrender to it. It is then that we start to loosen the hold of the ego.

It may seem more practical to follow the ego and have no principles to adhere to. However, when you really love yourself, you act from a different viewpoint. You act from love, not fear. Because you love yourself you automatically love other people, so there are now different issues to consider when making plans. You now ask yourself questions like: Is my decision beneficial for me as well as for all concerned? Is my decision serving the higher good of everybody? Am I striving to a win/win situation? This requires soul searching and at times poses difficult questions—and what's more, it may seem to delay or even compromise your own goal. So no wonder that for people who want a quick fix this is not very appealing. It is too much effort. Too much fuss.

Egocentric people often act in self-destructive ways because they do not believe in the mirror effect. If we realise that all events in our life are shaped by our inner concepts, and that, just like a mirror, external circumstances always reflect mental attitudes, it is easier to appreciate the importance of practising self-love as a powerful tool of personal growth.

Self-love is an ongoing practice. Cultivating self-love is like tending a bonfire, which, unless kept constantly fed with twigs and branches, will die out. So must we, in our relationships with our loved ones and ourselves, feed the light of love by showing compassion, by communicating with loving kindness, and by offering support, care and encouragement. The practice of self-love leads to personal growth. And no matter how high we grow, there are always higher peaks to reach for.

Self-love does not come easy. A comedian once remarked that it is much easier to love the entire humanity as a whole, rather than your next door neighbour. Self-love takes inner

8

work, determination, persistence and patience. You have to keep telling yourself over and over that you are lovable simply because you were created by a loving creator. Love therefore is your essence. To promote self-love and self-acceptance you must alter your concepts. You must let go of your own resentments and fears by refining your ego. And how do you refine your ego? I once heard someone say, 'If you want to change a person, treat him as if he has already changed.' If you view yourself as a changed person, if you deliberately focus your attention on your higher traits, on how good, strong, loving and lovable you are, your lower traits will wither from lack of attention. Think about what you love most about yourself. Forgive yourself a faulty behaviour. An expansion of self-love can help heal unloving attitudes, from self-abuse to overeating and from alcoholism to drug addiction.

Humanity needs more self-love. Too many people are defeating themselves with self-disapproval. Too many people act as their own worst enemies by self-mistreatment and self-abuse. But this is not just their private problem. Anything anyone does has an impact on others beyond a personal level because we are all parts of a collective consciousness. We all breathe the same air and walk the same earth. At a certain level, what you do affects me also, even if we live in different continents. We all share a common responsibility to benefit humanity by increasing our own self-love.

How can we increase self-love? The first step is to discard self-criticism and embrace self-acceptance. We all have a deep inner yearning to be loved instinctively, not to be analysed rationally. But the many perfectionists among us are obsessive fault-finders and must change their concepts to realise that we are always perfect and lovable for the present moment. In a future time, when we evolve and act differently, we will be perfect for that future moment. The

9

struggle for 'perfection' is a killer of self-love. It is always amazing to read in the newspapers about some of the most attractive movie stars, admired by millions all over the world, who dislike their appearance.

Unconditional self-approval is the first step because it leads you to improve your self-image and develop a more loving relationship with yourself. Start by contemplating on something you like about your body or personality, about something you did or said, about any accomplishment, however small. The more often you do it, the more you expand self-love. The tendency to spot personal flaws and dwell on them prevents many people from liking themselves. 'How can I love myself?' a person may ask, 'I'm stupid, fat, clumsy and insecure. I am a loser.' These are some of the excuses given by people who are not aware of their divine identity.

Overweight people are particularly prone to dislike and berate their bodies. They think that the underlying cause is lack of self-discipline or weak will-power, whereas the real cause is usually deep-seated fear. The fear of the ego. In many cases it is feelings of insecurity that make their bodies protect themselves by putting on extra layers of flab, with no thought to the amount of calories consumed. But then, love is about unconditional acceptance. As much as it may seem difficult for overweight people to accept their corpulent body, the initial step in any weight-loss plan is to start loving your body as it is right now. You can still aspire for a leaner figure by visualising your body shaping itself, but for now you love your body as it is. To quote Hermes Trimegistus, the great sage of antiquity, 'If you hate your body, my child, you cannot love yourself.' Love is about rising above personality limitations. And the first step in the journey of self-love is the practice of self-approval.

We live in a system of polarities. Everything has its opposite. And for a reason. How would we recognise beauty if there was no ugliness? How would we know right if there was no wrong? In fact, without plus and minus there would be no electrical power. Likewise, we have both opposites. There is a saint and a sinner within each of us. We each have our ego and our higher self and at different times we may find, much to our surprise, that we play both roles. Once we realise this predicament, it is important to forgive and accept ourselves just as we are. As we do, we heal our consciousness because forgiveness is a healing energy.

Humility is a great attribute of our higher loving self. Humility does not imply lack of self-confidence, but, rather, a deep awareness of self-worth. 'The meek shall inherit the earth' is a biblical confirmation that humility is an expression of inner power. Truly evolved people who are normally quiet and poised express their inner power through humbleness. They never try to impress or convince and yet have a great positive influence on people who seek their advice. Humility demonstrates a deep faith and an open heart.

Self-love can be enhanced by opening our hearts, learning to accept all parts of our personality, including the so-called 'faulty' parts that we dislike. We all have our humanity and our divinity. And our journey to enlightenment is about evolving our humanity and raising it to a higher level of consciousness. True love is unconditional. If we love conditionally, make a stipulation or attach strings to it, it is no longer a genuine love. In the words of an Indian guru: 'We don't love and live it there. We want something in return. This is not love. This is trade.'

Love your vices as well as your virtues. Love your fears and inadequacies as much as you love your higher feelings of courage, wisdom and peace. Love all your human flaws. Know that as you do, they will have less power over you. Hating your 'imperfections', resenting your negative thoughts and feelings, only serves to lock them deeper in your nature. Love is a powerful healing energy. Positive thoughts are much stronger than negative thoughts; one loving thought can cancel out hundreds of negative ones. You can use the tremendous power of love for your benefit. Sending love to your lower traits helps to heal them by raising their energy level to higher frequencies of spiritual vibration. In other words, loves raises a lower consciousness to a higher consciousness. The vibrations of higher consciousness are expressed also as a safeguarding light. The light of love is a great protective energy. In difficult or risky situations, radiate love. Its energy can help protect you by raising the vibration of lower, harmful energies, transforming them to higher auspicious ones. Love upgrades 'bad' energies to 'good' energies.

It is important to realise that what we label as good or bad, love or hate, are all made up of the same energy. Bad, hate or fear are lower vibrations of this energy, whereas good, love and joy are its higher vibrations. Imagine water as a basic energy. When cooled down to freezing point, it solidifies. It becomes a cool, dense ice. It takes the form of the lower energy level of water. When the same water is heated up it turns into a sublime, free-flowing vapour, which is the water's higher energetic expression. Likewise in human life, we use the warmth of love to raise the vibration of the cold 'hate', and upgrade it to a high vibration energy of warmth and love. The realisation of a common energy behind everything can help us overcome criticism and separation and promote an awareness of oneness and connectedness.

Life is not simple. Our bodies and minds are extremely complex. However, unlike a modern domestic appliance, we do not come into this world with an instruction manual. We have to learn on the go. And 'experience' is the name that we call our blunders. To benefit from our experiences, however, it helps to remember the words of Aldous Huxley:

'Experience is not what happens to you; it is what you do with what happens to you.'

Life experiences may appear daunting, and no wonder that we often become overly self-protective. We want assurances against pain. But life is not an insurance policy. Life is an adventure. We forget the teachings of the ancient Greek philosophers: *Live riskily.* Life requires us to show courage, to seek challenges, to take chances. And in this sense, self-love is a powerful tool which helps overcome fear and increase our trust in life while on the learning path. I was a young soldier when I was called to participate in a guard of honour during a military funeral of a young officer. The sad sight of the grieving young wife and her child crying at the burial broke something in me and tears were gushing from my eyes. The whole situation was very distressing. From then on, I mentally decided to protect myself and never again go to a cemetery, let alone attend any funeral. Little did I know about the system of duality that operates in the universe: That you cannot have one without the other. That you cannot have a rose without a thorn. Or in the words of Golda Meir, the late prime minister of Israel, 'Those who do not know how to weep with their whole heart don't know how to laugh either.'

We are here to learn and evolve. Our lifetime is a journey of discovery, and if we keep seeking the inner meaning of life's emotional upheavals, we will eventually discover that of the two basic emotions of love and fear, only love is real. We are each sent individual lessons, according to our specific needs which were predetermined by our souls before we were incarnated. At the root of each painful experience, there is a hidden message that needs to be understood and assimilated, in order for us to grow and evolve to the next level. The more painful the experience, the more salutary the lesson. Critical situations serve to teach life-changing lessons. And, as in any school, we can

13

choose whether to learn our lessons or to ignore them at our expense. We each learn in our own individual way and at our pace. We must therefore never compare ourselves to others to see how well we are faring. We are each unique, valuable and incomparable. It is enough for us to know that we are doing the best we can.

The lessons which come through minor adversities are initially very gentle. It is when we choose to ignore our inner guidance, our intuitive messages, that they become major crises. At first we are nudged gently and if we don't listen we are hit by a sledgehammer. Your higher self can create a cold to force you to take a much-needed rest. Longer illnesses give you an opportunity to release old erroneous attitudes and adopt more loving ones. You may need to learn to respect your needs better. This is not a punishment. The universe is just trying to get your attention and lead you to a higher level of self-love. And do not worry about your ability to cope. God does not dump on you more than you can handle.

I can still remember repeating the same faulty pattern of behaviour over and over. At times, I used to play the victim, only to discover that, as a result, I was being taken advantage of, until one day, I got so fed up I felt I simply could not take it any more. I felt a strong urge of inner rebellion. I said to myself, 'This is ludicrous. How much longer will I keep repeating the same attitude and put up with the same painful consequences? Isn't it time I learned the lesson?' And that was my turning point. Einstein once said that it is utter stupidity to keep doing the same things and expect different results. Many of us keep on doing just that because we are so set in our ways. And adopting new concepts and habits has never been easy. But we all learn to be loving and assertive at our own pace. We all change when we feel a shift from within, an impulse that becomes a watershed in our growth path. The good news is, though, that once a lesson is understood and integrated, once it becomes part of our consciousness, it is not repeated again.

Although many people choose chaos in their lives, the world is not chaotic. It operates according to specific laws that apply to every activity in life. These laws work for us or against us, depending on how we choose to use them. For example:

- The law of cause and effect—every action creates a reaction.
- The law of attraction—we attract experiences which reflect our concepts.
- The law of identification—whatever we identify with, we become.
- The law of increase—whatever we focus our attention on increases in our lives.
- The law of giving and receiving—it is as we give that we receive.

We are each a channel of divine love in a universe of law and order, and to channel well, let us imagine that we are each a water hose. As long as there is no kink in the hose, the water flows freely. It is only when the hose gets twisted that the flow stops. Our job is to keep these 'kinks'—our mental resistances and fears—out of our thinking and let the divine guidance flow. As Ralph Waldo Emerson said, 'We have to get our bloated nothingness out of the way of the divine circuit.' Calming our restless mind chatter, spending time alone, meditating or taking a walk in the woods are some of the activities that we can use to keep our channel clear. It is only in inner silence that we are able to hear our divine wisdom and develop self-love and all-embracing love, with which we can heal our souls and make our life work.

There is no difficulty that enough love
will not conquer;
no disease enough love will not heal;
no door that enough love will not open.
It makes no difference how deeply
seated may be the trouble; how hopeless
the outlook;
how muddled the tangle; how great
the mistake.

A sufficient realization of love
will dissolve it all.
If only you could love enough
you could be the happiest and most
powerful being in the world.

(Emmett Fox)

2

Self-Love: The Launch Pad to Universal Love

Why is self-love a prerequisite for universal love? Simple. The way you relate to yourself determines the way you relate to other people. When you are gentle and compassionate with yourself, you are gentle and compassionate with others. Self-love is the foundation for universal love; in fact, they are indistinguishable from each other. According to Dr M. Scott Peck in his classic book *The Road Less Traveled*: 'We are incapable of loving another unless we love ourselves. We cannot be a source of strength unless we nurture our own strength.' We can therefore only love another person as much as we love ourselves.

Love is the wisdom of the heart. It is a way to refine the soul. It is a way to flow with life rather than resist it. Self-love is our connection to the universe because love is the energy that runs it. It leads us to realise that our own love is part of an infinite loving power which sustains us moment by moment; a loving power which is constantly leading us to our higher good; an infinitely intelligent power that always gives us what is perfectly right for us, not necessarily what we think we want; a power which is good and wise in what it gives and what it denies.

Love opens our heart. It releases compassion, humility, patience and forgiveness, virtues that make our life flow

17

more smoothly and happily. Self-love reminds us of our divine identity if we stoop to feel jealous or lesser than any other person. We learn to rejoice in another's success, knowing that it is possible for us too as we are all equally loved and provided for by the infinite abundance of providence.

When we nurture our self-love we promote our sense of worthiness and lead a more fulfilled life. We finally come to realise that our self-love is a reflection of God's love for us; that the universe is always there for us to grant our higher good. We only must be open to receive. To obtain your wishes, simply tell yourself that as a child of God, you are naturally entitled to them. Do not strive to manipulate issues. Do not push your luck; *trust* your luck.

Falun Gong, an ancient Chinese philosophical system of spiritual cultivation for improving body, mind and spirit by meditation and exercise which is currently sweeping the world, teaches that the universe operates on three fundamental principles: truthfulness, compassion and forbearance. These qualities are claimed to be inherent in every atom and molecule and to govern every aspect of the universe. In order to grow, says master Li Hongzhi, who introduced this system to the public in 1992, one must align with these principles and act out of truthfulness, compassion and forbearance, virtues which virtually constitute love. In fact, these are also the same divine attributes of God as frequently described in the Bible. It seems as if the universal truth is one, no matter which culture it comes from.

Self-love teaches us to be the source of love, rather than wait for others to love us first. Self-love leads us to universal love because when we learn to really accept ourselves unconditionally, we automatically stop criticising other people. With self-acceptance, it is also easier to accept others without censure. Self-love is a far-reaching energy. It beams out of us to make a contribution to others. When you act with self-acceptance, self-love and self-respect, you not only evolve yourself but you inspire others to grow by setting an example.

In the school of life, our relationships with other people are in fact workshops for our own evolution. Relationships open the way to ultimate love, teaching us to love the virtuous and the sinner alike. When asked about his Chinese enemies who invaded Tibet, the Dalai Lama said: 'Without enemy, how can we learn tolerance? How can we learn patience?' Difficult people are our private tutors. Difficult situations are actually challenging us to become more loving and more trusting. Our spiritual maturity is eventually epitomised by the ability to accept people who are different from us.

It is easier to love unconditionally when we realise that an offensive behaviour often hides a fearful soul. Fear breeds aggressiveness. Personal conflicts and national wars are triggered by non-loving feelings such as fear, insecurity, revenge or greed. Conversely, a non-judgemental consciousness promotes peace of mind. It helps us become transparent to the negative energies of other people, letting these energies flow through us without hitting any inner cord. It helps avoid suffering.

All painful relationships, all break-ups, crises and predicaments, in fact all things that we may perceive as misfortunes, are gifts. They all have inherent benefits. They are opportunities to go deeper, listen to our inner voice and evolve. The universe works in perfect ways and everything that happens is perfect. Every event, big or small, has a good reason. There are no coincidences. Everything that happens to us is designed for our good by a higher, loving intelligence. In hindsight, you may look back at your life and realise how past failures, setbacks or adversities that you once worried sick about enabled you to let go of a flawed emotion that pestered you, or opened up new options that changed your life for the better. If you sit still and listen to your inner messages, every situation can provide you with insights that can lead to deeper understandings.

Meditation is one of the best ways to listen to your higher self. By calming your mind chatter and creating silent intervals between thoughts, meditation opens the way to contact your inner wisdom, your connection to divine intelligence. Through flashes of insights and whispers, urges and feelings, meditation can gradually lead you to perceive the real meaning of events in your life, the story behind the story if you will, from a higher perspective. It reveals the moral behind any occurrence and cycle, the reason a relationship was formed and the reason it broke down; how and why you attracted these situations to yourself and in what way they served your higher good. Meditation, however, is a reflective attitude and can be done in different ways to suit everyone, even those who are not inclined to formally sit and meditate. Anything that enables you to relax, silence your thoughts and concentrate, even during daily activities, is a meditation; focusing your attention on anything you do, even when washing dishes, can be a meditation. Similarly, a long walk in the park is a fine example of 'walking meditation'. All forms of meditation connect you to your higher wisdom.

So dare to take the leap of faith. Start by trusting that anything you do, and anything that happens to you, is designed for your higher good, even if you cannot understand why. As the Bible commands, 'Trust in the Lord with all thine heart and lean not to thine own understanding' (Proverbs 3:5). Keep trusting, even if it looks as though things are going downhill, and people you are attracted to are backing away. It serves no purpose to torment yourself by imagining worst-possible case scenarios in your mind over and over. Love yourself enough to cease this self-torture and contemplate on the brighter side of things. Realise that painful situations are an opportunity to develop more faith in the higher scheme of things. Failures are often precursors of victories. In fact, you must be lost before you can be found. As the famous 'Amazing Grace' hymn goes, 'I once was lost but now I'm found, was blind but now I see.'

Most of us, though, need to go all the way down in our personal life, to actually hit rock-bottom, before we are able to change inhibiting concepts such as insecurity or low self-worth and rise to higher levels of loving assertiveness. Many need to be losers before they become winners. Failures, however, are not losses, they are only growth lessons meant to make us stronger, wiser and more loving. According to Donald Nichol in his book *Holiness*, 'we cannot lose once we realise that everything that happens to us has been designed to teach us holiness'. There are no losers among those of us who choose to change their concepts and evolve. Anyone trudging along the growth path is a guaranteed winner. So don't victimise yourself. Instead of seeing your-self as a victim in hiding, visualise yourself as a victor in waiting.

To love is to cooperate with God. Love is a form of worship. According to the teaching of the Indian avatar, Sai Baba, 'God is love and love is God. Where there is love there is God. Love more people more and love them more intensely. Transform love into service. Transform service into worship. That is the highest spiritual practice.' Let us therefore open up to the love that we actually are, to lead us to enlightenment.

'Where there is love there is life,' said Mahatma Gandhi. Love is the sustaining energy of life which keeps us alive and well. The only reason humanity has prevailed despite incredibly widespread evil throughout history is because love always surpassed hatred. Human life is supported by

21

the same loving energy that makes trees grow and birds sing, just as a baby is nurtured by his mother's love, because without love, a baby can literally die. We are loved unconditionally by our souls and by the universe. In fact, if only we were able to realise how much the higher powers love us, we would never feel fearful; we would never feel alone and we would never worry. Imagine being surrounded by a loving presence. Merge with it. It will make you feel better no matter what your situation is.

The whole universe is one interconnected love story. Love is maintained through an interaction between people. No one is totally self-sufficient. We all play a part in each other's life. Have you ever stopped to consider how many people had to labour in order for you to enjoy your morning coffee or daily bread roll? From the farmers, packers and truck drivers to the millers, roasters and bakers, we take this interconnectedness for granted without realising that we are all linked up by a loving connection. Nothing can exist without this universal loving interaction.

The principle of oneness of humanity and the connectedness of all life is a sacred tenet in ancient Jewish tradition. In one of the final emotional scenes of the movie *Schindler's List*, when the war has just ended and Schindler addresses his liberated workers outside the plant to bid them farewell before fleeing, he is presented by his manager with a gold ring which has a Hebrew engraving from the Talmud: 'He who saves one life saves the world entire.'

Adopting the concept of oneness, believing that we are each part of the same whole, is one of the best ways to increase both self-love and universal love. We need to realise that we are all godly because our souls are individualised parts of God; despite our physical appearance, we are all actually spiritual beings. When you finally realise that you are an incarnated spirit, it becomes easier to love, accept and appreciate yourself and others. We all share the same planet and breathe the same air. We are all fellow travellers in the journey to enlightenment.

We are here to heal our spirit and realise that painful relationship experiences are of our own making. They are all lessons designed by our souls, each with a specific message to convey. We actually attract various teachers, both tormentors and benefactors. So there is really no one to blame. Growing is learning to assume responsibility for anything that happens. The universe knows that we are here to discover the truths that we each need in order to evolve. And it knows that we all do the best we can in every eventuality, even if it seems that we blunder. If we knew better we would have done better. So why criticise? Why blame? When we choose self-love, we learn to accept the undesirable and the unacceptable. We thus learn to claim our true power.

Self-love is reflected in many ways. It is expressed by validation, support, compassion and forgiveness. Respecting your needs, valuing yourself and your time, releasing your past by loving it, doing the things you enjoy, allowing your prosperity, abstaining from self-abuse, pursuing your happiness and releasing fear—these are all expressions of self-love. When you are more loving to yourself, you help lessen emotional suffering during painful experiences. When you really love yourself you realise that offending yourself is as sinful as offending other people. According to the late Ken Keyes Jr. in *Handbook to Higher Consciousness*, 'You add suffering to the world just as much when you take offence as when you give offence.' It is the intention of a loving universe for all people to be successful and happy. And by pursuing love and happiness you are aligning with the divine will. You are on the road to creating your own bliss.

The way we treat our shortcomings is commonly misconstrued. Many people become extremely self-critical when they realise they did something wrong for which they constantly berate themselves. They simply won't let go, they won't forgive and forget. In such instances, they feel they are not good enough and, therefore, not worthy of love. Well, mistakes are part of our human nature. As the saying goes, to err is human, to forgive is divine. Forgiveness does not give you carte blanche to start sinning again. It just gives you an opportunity to start afresh and do it right. Do not be discouraged if you keep repeating the same errors and making the same wrong choices again and again. We all learn lessons at our own pace. We may resent past mistakes and bad choices. But resenting our past can only serve to lock it deeper in our aura and attract more of the same since, according to the law of attraction, like attracts like.

We all have a side to us that we do not like. Many pretend it does not exist. The more we deny it, though, the stronger it becomes. Over time, it gets so strong that it can absorb us and we become the person we have always dreaded. Evolved people learn to be honest with themselves and say, 'OK, there is a little bit of me that is not perfect, but there is also much bigger side of me that is a nice person.' At this point of self-acceptance, an integration takes place. We accept ourselves as we are, and get on with the business of improving our lives.

A better way to release a resentment, a grudge or the impression of an unhappy experience is by lovingly accepting it. You may have lost a job or a relationship and feel hurt. Let go. Release your hurts with love and do not carry any emotional baggage into the future. Mentally say to whoever wronged you: 'I bless you with love and release you from my life.' Forgiveness has a great healing power. *A Course in Miracles* states: 'When you feel sick, look around you to see who it is you need to forgive.' In the Judaeo-Christian tradition, a request for forgiveness is a common prayer. We ask God to forgive our iniquities as we forgive

24

others. Blame blocks you emotionally. Forgiveness sets you free.

Developing a non-judgemental attitude towards other people is easier when we come to recognise that our own consciousness is a fragment of the same oneness that Carl Jung called *collective unconscious*, which may explain sporadic flashes of intuition, when sometimes we are astonished to find out that we know something without knowing where from; when we get an inexplicable urge to make a snap decision that is eventually vindicated.

Every person has a right to be here. Saints and sinners alike. Even the most unlovable, even the so-called 'low life' share this right. Every life has a meaning. Everyone is here according to a higher plan and each contributes to this plan in his or her way. You may question the contribution of a person who behaves in an evil way, since evil represents anti-love and darkness. But unwittingly, evil serves a purpose too. It serves to warn others away from its pitfalls. It teaches other people to be more aware, more conscious and more loving. As Kahlil Gibran wrote: 'I've learned silence from the talkative, toleration from the intolerant and kindness from the unkind; yet strange, I'm ungrateful to those teachers.' In fact, as you learn to accept other people for who they are, your concepts will eventually rise beyond the polarities of 'good' and 'bad'. When you meet people who behave in a way you disapprove of, you will think of them as 'different'. Variety is the spice of life. Imagine what a dull place the world would be if everyone agreed on everything.

The futility of criticising other people in a self-righteous way becomes apparent when we realise that we actually attract people and circumstances into our lives which, in one way or another, reflect our own traits. The German philosopher Hermann Hesse said, 'If you hate a person, you hate something in him that is part of yourself. What isn't part of ourselves does not bother us.' Many centuries earlier the Jewish Talmud declared, 'He who condemns others, condemns through his own fault.'

All too often we forget our common identity, our brotherhood. We judge people by their appearances. If we like their looks we can forgive them almost anything; if we don't, we blame them for almost everything. That is when we close off our hearts and minds. That is when we become resentful and fearful, until something happens to wake us up and remind us about our collective connection. Suppose you have been stuck in a traffic jam for twenty minutes when it starts moving again at a snail's pace. You suddenly see another car in which a woman is signalling that she wants to get into your lane ahead of you. You can think, 'I have been stuck here all this time, why can't she wait too?' Or, you can remember your common identity and think, 'It is my sister who is in distress and needs help.' When you mentally separate yourself from people you resent, you are also separating yourself from people you revere.

Actually, criticising others impedes your own ability to love yourself unconditionally. When you do not accept other people as they are unless their behaviour complies with what you think is 'right', you are sending a message to your unconscious mind that you can only accept yourself conditionally, only when you are at your best, but not at your worst.

We affect each other with our emotions. True, I will not bleed if you cut your finger and you will not feel my pain when I hurt. Yet, with a loving look we can have a big impact on each other. If you smile at someone, he or she may smile at someone else. If that person is inspired to send a cheerful email, your smile may surround the world. The same goes for negativity. If you frown at someone and they pass it on, who knows what mishap your frown may lead to.

Our power to affect people was beautifully illustrated in

the movie *Pay it Forward*, with Kevin Spacey portraying Mr Simonet, a social studies school teacher of eleven-year-old seventh graders in Las Vegas. Mr Simonet is an avant-garde educator. He inspires unconventional thinking. From day one he starts asking the children soul-searching questions such as, 'What does the world mean to you?' 'What does the world expect from you?' In the first lesson he presents the kids with a challenging assignment: to come up with ideas of how to change the world for the better. One emotionally sensitive child, Trevor, is deeply moved. He comes up with the 'pay it forward' idea, a utopian concept that uses the dormant power of goodness within each individual to affect other people. Instead of paying someone back for a previous favour, as is normally done, this idea goes a step further. 'Pay it forward' exceeds altruism. It motivates a person to take the initiative to go out seemingly for no reason, and do three favours to three strangers who need help. These people, in turn, become morally obligated to pass on the buck and help out three other individuals, allowing the flow of loving energy to grow and multiply exponentially, thus making a great difference in the world. The movie shows many heart-warming situations which illustrate how the flow of unimpeded love-energy creates a chain reaction and transforms people's lives. Eventually, this idea spreads like fire and in a few months becomes a national movement.

Love is a mysterious emotion. It is far too complex and far too large to have a single definition. Love comes in various forms and besides, each person has his or her own concept of what constitutes love. But regardless of your own specific understanding, love has one common factor: When you love, you feel more alive, more expanded. Real love, however, is more than uncontrollable emotion. Actually, it takes a conscious decision to practise love. It takes a willingness to be vulnerable. It takes a determination to keep your heart open and accept people as they are. Accepting not only their virtues but also their 'imperfections'. And by dissolving all separateness, you help yourself and others to evolve to higher levels of unconditional love.

In fact, our human imperfections, which we commonly tend to condemn or ignore, give meaning to our life because they provide us with a mission to grow and evolve to higher levels of self-refinement. It is only when we acknowledge our blind spots that we can transform them to higher traits by shining on them the light of our higher awareness.

We do not have to do anything to validate our being. We do not have to work hard to earn the right to eat. In fact, to evolve and prosper in our hectic society, we need to stop doing so much and set aside time to be still, meditate and practise 'beingness', because it is in our peaceful solitude that we can hear our inner guidance. I once heard a workaholic say, 'I feel I need to work hard to justify my existence.' This is the fearful voice of the ego. Our souls know that each one of us is here for a higher reason. All you need to do to justify your existence is to practise love in daily life.

The way of the soul is opposite to that of the ego. Instead of being linear, it is cyclical and sequential. The soul evolves and heals us through cycles of events in our personal life, in our relationships and our careers. Cycles come and go. Some are more painful while others are more pleasant. Some are longer and some are shorter. Most of them, however, may be incomprehensible to our intellect during the time they happen because our minds think linearly. Our intellect can only reason events that make sense to our rationale—that is, events that go in straight logical line from A to B. Cycles, however, are much more convoluted and complex. They may include inexplicable chains of events and seemingly unrelated sequences of ups and downs. They can span various periods of time in which spontaneous occurrences and miraculous coincidences happen with perfect timing in order to bring about a predestined outcome.

It is not easy to predict the final result of a cycle by analysing things rationally. People normally want things to make sense in a logical and realistic way. When, during a cycle, people think 'realistically' about the problems at hand and how insurmountable they seem, they are actually being pessimistic, since the logical mind cannot foresee unexpected lucky breaks, chance meetings or windfalls that seem to come out of the blue. The mind cannot fathom how parts of a cycle, like pieces of a puzzle, fit together. It cannot see the higher picture of a cycle as it unfolds. Cycles baffle the intellect, which is why people say that God works in mysterious ways. This is the time when faith in the higher power is needed most. Faith in an infinite wisdom which is orchestrating the cycle for our higher good. A relationship or career impasse can be a blessing in disguise if you use it to bolster your faith by repeating to yourself over and over the fact that God can make a way where there is no way. All cycles are necessary stages for our growth. It is only in hindsight that we can realise how a painful experience that we once fretted about actually opened up new beginnings and taught us a much-needed lesson.

Once the lesson has been integrated, the concept of self-love can be extended to others. It is easier to enhance our love towards other people as we develop a non-judgemental consciousness—that is, accepting people without passing judgement. If everyone is a divinity, and divinity is beyond judgement, how can we judge the divine? We are each a living deity. For centuries Indian gurus were telling us to see God in every person we meet. When you see people in the street, in the workplace, in a supermarket or in the post office, try to see beyond their physical bodies. Visualise people as souls. As the Sufis say, 'See with your heart.' You may be surprised to feel how practising this attitude can help you increase unconditional acceptance of others. Babies keep some affinity with their previous soul state from which they recently arrived. They still have a natural sense of connectedness which is gradually lost later in childhood as ego and individual identity are developed. It is very important to redevelop an awareness of oneness with all mankind. Jesus wore a seamless tunic to symbolise the cohesion and unity of humanity.

Humanity can be likened to a human body where each cell represents a person. In this metaphor, the six billion people on this earth symbolise the sixty trillion cells in each human body. Like people, each cell has its own identity and its own unique functions while still being a part of a whole. Each cell performs billions of things every second while knowing exactly what other cells are doing and interacting with them. Through very intricate but harmonious processes this cellular intelligence enables the body to sustain overall health and vitality. Likewise, humanity could benefit as a whole if each of us would do his or her job while lovingly cooperating with others harmoniously.

Emotional baggage is a major obstacle to self-love. Feelings of guilt, resentment and grudges, regrets about missed chances and doubts about our divine identity all block our way to spiritual growth. So how can we go about releasing these inhibitions? Louise Hay, author of *You Can Heal Your Life*, recommends looking at the mirror and saying to your reflection in the glass, I love you. As simple as this exercise may first seem, it is a powerful means of releasing pent-up grievances, bitterness and traumas that sit in our aura and inhibit our growth. This exercise can be an emotionally cathartic experience because it faces you directly with the core of your erroneous concepts. It confronts you with repressed emotions that you would rather forget and disown. It allows to surface painful memories of past experiences, when you followed your ego and acted in unloving, fearful or aggressive ways. It can bring tears, sadness and regrets. But this catharsis is healing. When it is over, it can raise you to a higher level of self-love and improve your ability to become a whole person. Alcoholics Anonymous beautifully illustrate the effect of the mirror concept with their poem 'The Man in the Glass':

When you get what you want in your struggle for self
And the world makes you king for a day,
Just go to the mirror and look at yourself
And see what the man has to say.

For it isn't your father or mother or wife
Who judgement upon you must pass;
The fellow whose verdict counts most in your life
Is the one staring back from the glass.

Some people may think you a straight-shootin' chum
And call you a wonderful guy.
But the man in the glass says you're only a bum
If you can't look him straight in the eye.

He's the fellow to please, never mind all the rest.
For he is with you right up to the end.
And you've passed your most dangerous, difficult test
If the man in the glass is your friend.

You may fool the whole world down the pathway of
    life
And get pats on your back as you pass.
But your final reward will be heartaches and tears
If you've cheated the man in the glass.

Life is often described as a journey to enlightenment. I like to imagine us all trying to climb a mountain, the infinite mountain of divine consciousness, on our way to higher peaks of awareness. Ascending the mountain is not easy.

31

We sometimes falter; we sometimes trip over a cliff and lose our footing; occasionally, we get tired and take a pause; and every so often we might even lose our balance and roll down to a lower cliff. But when we get to a higher peak, we can sit and rest for a while, looking at the progress we have made, enjoying our achievement in reaching a higher perspective of awareness. This is our reward for going through life's ordeals.

Focused attention is concentrated energy, and whatever issue we choose to pay attention to is energised and increased. This is also known as the law of increase. It means that when you think about your doubts and fears, when you spend time castigating yourself in a non-loving way, you are actually intensifying your lower nature. You are deepening the very shortcomings you would like to get rid of. But when you concentrate your attention on your virtues, your lower traits will simply shrivel from lack of attention. Criticising and resenting yourself and others is not only futile, it is counter-productive. Therefore, count your blessings. Tell yourself repeatedly how good, able, successful and lucky you are. Affirm it in the present tense. Feel it as an undisputable fact. If done with conviction, your behaviour will automatically start reflecting these affirmations, in a similar way to the way it obeys hypnotic suggestions.

Spiritual growth is, in a way, like bodybuilding. To develop muscles, we go to the gym for a workout. We need to push against weights which symbolise obstacles. This means constant work. This means going within to our spiritual gym. This means learning to accept the flow of life with all its twists and turns. And when we have to go through a major crisis which is forcing our hand, it helps to remember the words of Kahlil Gibran in *Sand and Foam*: 'One may not reach the dawn save by the path of the night.' Upgrading your perceptions and deepening your awareness

32

that everything happens for a reason will raise your spirit to a higher level of vibration. And the higher the vibration, the better the things that will be attracted to you.

The problem is that it takes time. During this journey, our spirit may evolve quicker than our personality. We can find that one day we act with confidence, love and acceptance, while the next day we are ravaged by doubts and fear. It is very important not to push yourself beyond your fear. A friend may ask you repeatedly for a favour, yet you feel you are being used or abused. Nevertheless, instead of asserting yourself and saying no, you choose not to respect your feelings and, instead, yield. You agree to go against your better judgement and live to regret it and to berate yourself for being a wimp. To avoid guilt feelings in compromising situations, however, it is important to realise that any decision you sincerely make while obeying your inner voice will eventually be also for the higher good of the other person. This is because our higher selves are all connected harmoniously at soul levels.

Integrating personality behaviour with our inner truth can be a lengthy process. It is time to be patient. With patience and perseverance, with courage and persistence, the time will come when we suddenly feel a shift from within; an erroneous concept held for too long will have changed; we will start to see the world in a different light. This is the sign that we have assimilated the lesson, making it part of us. We can then enjoy the fruits of our achievement, of having grown to a higher level of love and happiness.

'If you would learn the secret of right relations;
Look only for the divine in people and things,
And leave the rest to God.'

From *Kinship with all Life*
by J. Allen Boone

3

The Law of Cause and Effect

'You reap what you sow' does not apply to farming only. It is a universal law of human life. Hence, a self-loving person would most likely choose to plant flowers in the garden of his mind, rather than thorns. Many people generally believe that this is true. Most people however do not realise how deep down this principle goes, how definite it is. 'What's the great harm in a little white lie to spare someone's feelings? What if I said I was a loser? What if I said I never get things right? I did not mean it anyway.' How can a little self-abasing remark that I have blurted out absent-mindedly come back to haunt me, many would wonder.

Yet just like the law of gravity, the law of cause and effect is absolute. It has no exceptions. It operates on large scales as well as on minuscule ones. The law is documented repeatedly throughout the Bible. For example, Chapter 62 of the book of Psalms states, 'thou renderest to every man according to his work'. This means that the law of cause and effect operates separately from the merciful nature of the universe. In this law, compassion, pity and forgiveness do not apply, because it asserts that like attracts like. As the old saying goes, life may not be just but it is exact. Regardless of any wishful thinking, what you sow is exactly what you reap. If you have sown thorns, do not expect roses.

The law of cause and effect impacts every aspect of our

life, from finances and relationships to health and happiness. As Ralph Waldo Emerson stated in his essay 'Spiritual Laws', 'Hidden away in the inner nature of the real man is the law of life and some day he will discover it and consciously make use of it. He will heal himself, make himself happy and prosperous and will live in an entirely different world for he will have discovered that life is from within and not from without.' For better or for worse, the thoughts we think and the words we say are the inner causes that draw outer effects.

The whole world operates on the principle of comeuppance. What goes around comes around. Any lie, scam or wrongdoing, however small, is accountable. Words have a tremendous power; what goes out in the form of words returns as experiences. Moreover, the mere intention to act either in a compassionate way or in a harmful way applies, since thoughts and emotions release powerful magnetic energies which attract corresponding events. Every moment, our thoughts, feelings and words are creating our reality. Nothing happens accidentally. When we realise the enormous power of thoughts and words to shape our lives, we will become more aware of our words and actions. We will want to think lovingly, speak lovingly and act lovingly. We will realise that the dramas in our lives reflect the mental turmoil in our minds. We will also strive for purity of mind by speaking only the truth. The nature of the soul is truthfulness and when we adhere to the truth, we align with our higher self.

Throughout the Bible truth is expounded as a sacred universal tenet, a principle by which the universe operates. 'God of Truth' is a common attribute of the Almighty. To live in truth means also keeping all your promises. Make a few promises, but the ones you do make, keep. Otherwise truth is violated. When you distort the truth, exaggerate it or compromise it, when you manipulate it in any way, you go against the principles of the universe. You are defiling your thoughts and just like a magnet, unclean thoughts always attract unfavourable experiences. When you work your way out of an embarrassing situation by making up little fibs and lies, even in jest, you are actually treating *yourself* with disrespect by deviating from your divine identity. With enough self-love and self-respect, however, you will have the courage to say the truth and treat yourself and others with dignity.

Acting in honesty does not mean lowering your guard or being a simpleton. We all know that life can sometimes be a complicated venture and acting as a sacrificial lamb is not self-love. But in awkward situations it is worth knowing what part of the truth to say and what part to hold back. Such situations offer us the opportunity to use the law of cause and effect to our advantage.

Nothing is inconsequential. If you bully, insult, cheat or steal and manage to get away with it, you have created a negative karma. You are debited in the divine ledger and to balance it out, you will have to suffer by attracting equally painful experiences.

Our unconscious mind has no sense of humour; it accepts every word we utter and every thought we think for what they are. Much like a computer, it registers everything as a default instruction. If you berate yourself—if you say, for example, 'How stupid of me'—stupidity is accepted as a mode of action, and much like a hypnotic suggestion, will come back to haunt you sooner or later. If you plan to cheat, con or abuse others, be prepared to experience personally similar incidents.

All thoughts and words are programmed for future operation under the law of cause and effect. Given time, every single statement becomes true. Each moment, your words and thoughts are creating your reality. If you want to change your situation for the better, start using positive terms in every phrase. Instead of saying, 'I'm a loser,' say, 'I did not succeed this time but I have learned a valuable lesson for next time.' The law of cause and effect is a neutral power, and when used properly for your good, it can be a powerful tool in shaping up a better future.

We have all heard about 'self-fulfilling prophecies', but we seldom take the concept seriously enough in every little thing we say. A friend of mine who moved into a new place had to remove a few floorboards in preparation for a gas plumbing job, and hired a carpenter to do the job. When the carpenter failed to show up on time, she got impatient and blurted angrily, 'I will take off these boards myself even if it kills me.' When she picked a hammer and a chisel and started pounding, she drove the chisel deep into her palm and ended with a scar for life. Sometimes the effect is swift. And the lesson is obvious: Be careful what you wish for.

Jesus understood this. He said, 'By thy words thou shalt be justified and by thy words thou shalt be condemned.' Words have a tremendous impact on our lives. They induce feelings that affect the experience of a person using them. It can take only a couple of words to either demoralise you or uplift you. When you feel moody, try saying *I feel wonderful*, slowly and with a deep conviction, three times. Don't you feel a little better? Naturally, you must say it with feeling and emotion regardless of present conditions and circumstances. It behoves us to use words that work for us rather than words which work against us.

Everything you think and imagine will be reflected in your reality. In the words of Donald Curtis, 'We are what and where we are because we have first imagined it.' That is why positive imagining and thinking is essential. Resentments, grudges and feelings of ill-will create a negative karma. They stay in our aura and attract similar types of energies. From the mischievous to the atrocious, these actions create a karmic debt which needs to be paid sooner or later, in one way or another, in order to achieve a state of balance, since the universe always strives to reach an energetic equilibrium. You can manipulate people but not the divine law. If you nicked a box of pencils from your office, do not be surprised if a cheque you were expecting gets lost in the mail.

When we realise that everything that happens to us is of our own making, it will be easier to assume responsibility for anything that occurs in our lives. We will stop blaming other people or God for our punishments. God does not punish. God is love. As *A Course in Miracles* states, 'God does not forgive because He has not condemned.'

On the other hand, acts of love or compassion, such as being kind to a stranger, forgiving an enemy, helping someone in need or praying for the sick, all create divine credit points. They attract beneficial effects in one form or another, which often come when least expected. The more you love yourself and the more compassionate you are to others, the higher you raise the frequency of your energy. And it is this higher frequency that attracts higher and better things into your life. Loving others is really a gift to yourself. It is an effortless way to become 'luckier'.

Self-love is a powerful tool in our quest for self-improvement and spiritual growth, since it too is governed by the law of cause and effect. With self-love, you will be careful not to abuse yourself in thought, word or action. With self-love you will automatically desire for yourself only the best and the highest and you will eventually attract the best and the highest. You can thus create your own heaven on earth. And as you learn to love yourself more you will prefer to grow through joyful experiences rather than through painful lessons. Once you realise that you actually reap what you sow, you will obviously prefer to sow in your mind only the most beneficial thoughts. You will cast love and blessings upon the waters and they shall come back to you multiplied.

Self-love is a magnetic energy. It has a powerful karma. As you love yourself you also draw to yourself the love of others, their help and their goodwill. As you respect and appreciate yourself, you will find that others start to respect you and value you. Likewise, if you feel unworthy, inadequate, fearful or insecure, do not be surprised if you find that friends are exploiting you and strangers are victimising you. Karma, as you know by now, works in both directions. Karma however imposes a great liability. It compels us to take responsibility for all our actions rather than falling into the common trap of accusing other people for any misfortune. By assuming responsibility, we can grow to a higher level of understanding and avoid undesirable things happening again in the future.

You need, however, to know your boundaries. You have to know where your individuality ends and wholeness begins. If you do not, others will invade your private space, just like a vulnerable country with no clear border markings, which attracts invaders. Trying to please others at all costs, constantly apologising, playing doormat and seeking approval from other people for your rightful actions all mean acting with no clearly defined boundaries. This attitude does not serve your growth. If you do not assert yourself, people will sense it and will try to encroach on your domain. They may bully you or demand things that you do not want to give. It is no use blaming them. They are only reflecting back to you, as a mirror, your own mental attitudes. It is you who is attracting these situations. It is the law of cause and effect in action.

Learning to say no to others may sometimes be daunting but it is part of self-love training. When you do not want to go along with other people, they may feel threatened and may try to gain control over you. They may use every trick in the book, such as accusations, emotional blackmail or power struggle. Keep cool. When this happens, just remember that their behaviour was actually attracted by the karma created by your fearful or unloving attitudes of mind. And don't blame yourself either. Stepping out of guilt is an important aspect of self-love and self-acceptance. Be grateful for the lesson they provided you and move on. Ultimately, everyone around you is your teacher. Every failure or setback offers you the opportunity to change perceptions. Disappointments can open your eyes to release limiting emotions that you have outgrown. Eventually, you stop clinging to things and ideas that do not serve your higher good any more. You learn to let go of any attachments to anything that makes you unhappy.

Personal crises are healing. Times of crises are opportunities. In Chinese, the word 'crisis' (*Wei-chi*) holds two meanings: danger and opportunity. True. Times of crisis may be extremely uncomfortable, terrifying and painful. We may lose a job or a relationship, we may contract a disease or go through a traumatic phase and feel as if our whole world has collapsed on us. In these difficult moments it helps to realise that crises usually signal a time of change; an opportunity to grow and upgrade our concepts; a chance to get stronger and evolve. Our soul has led us to this crisis because we are now ready to move on, to change course and rise to higher levels of achievement and happiness. The past is dying out to make way for the new. It is usually only in hindsight that we can realise how a painful experience was a blessing in disguise.

I can relate a typical example from my own personal life. Many years ago, during a visit to Amsterdam as a member of a delegation, I got a sore throat and my voice became husky. Since I was supposed to hold meetings the next day, I reluctantly went along with a friend's nagging suggestions to call a doctor. The hotel sent us a respectable-looking middle-aged doctor who diagnosed tonsillitis and decided to

40

give me a penicillin injection, to, in his words, 'kill my infection'. I told him I would prefer a mild antiseptic but he insisted on the jab without checking me first for a possible allergy. A week later I returned home to find itchy skin eruptions on my body and a rising temperature. My family doctor who came to see me found that I had developed an acute serum disease as a result of being extremely allergic to penicillin. I spent three months in bed hovering between life and death, with a high fever and an agonising itchy rash all over me. By the time I finally recovered, I had lost my trust in conventional medicine and decided from then on to assume responsibility for my own health.

This traumatic experience was to change the course of my life. I started to read anything I could find on nutrition and alternative therapies. I experimented with various disciplines such as vegetarianism, veganism and macrobiotics, to name a few. I was able to improve my health, but that was not enough. I decided to make nutrition my career. It took years but eventually I graduated as a doctor of nutrition. I became a successful nutritional consultant. I lectured, wrote articles and authored best-selling books which are still in print. Indeed, it was only in hindsight I could realise that my personal tribulations were meant for my higher good and to aid my ability to contribute to the well-being of others.

Life is mysterious. We can often see strange things that defy explanation happening around us to people. How can we explain a baby's cot death, birth defects, children's cancer and accidents happening at an early age, seemingly without a karmic reason? How can a baby or a tot have acquired such a massive karmic debt in their short lives? Why do some people seem as if they are doomed to suffer while others enjoy the carefree life of a playboy? Such questions remain unanswerable because we cannot know the soul's healing plan for anyone's lifetime, nor the karmas of past lives that need to be balanced out according to the law of cause and effect.

The Dalai Lama said that it is difficult to explain life's events from the narrow perspective of a single lifetime, since karmic debts such as abuses, hurts and unresolved issues of past lives which were not atoned for or healed are carried into the next ones to be redressed. The concept of our incarnation over many lifetimes is now rapidly becoming popular, as cases of near-death experiences and hypnotic regression therapies are proving. Books such as *Many Lives, Many Masters* by the noted Florida psychiatrist Dr Brian Weiss are creating changes in people's perceptions on life and death. They teach that birth is not the beginning and death is not the end. These ideas, however, are not new. Two thousand years ago Cicero said, 'The life of the dead rests in the remembrance of the living.'

In more recent times Carl Jung, the famous psychologist who joined modern psychology with spirituality, said, 'My life as I lived it has often seemed to me like a story that has no beginning and no end. I had the feeling that I was a historical fragment, an excerpt from which the preceding and succeeding text was missing. I could well imagine that I might have lived in former centuries and there encountered questions I was not yet able to answer; that I had to be born again because I had not fulfilled the task that was given to me.'

The concept that the law of cause and effect extends beyond lifetimes may be illustrated by the story a man who was keen to see a movie, and went to the cinema only to find out that he had arrived late and the film had started a while ago. He decided to buy a ticket anyway and got in. As he sat down, he was shocked by what he was watching. He saw a group of seemingly cruel thugs beating and torturing a helpless man. They pulled off his fingernails, stabbed his private parts with burning skewers, and used any other kind of atrocious torture they could think of. The late-arriving spectator became so unsettled and distressed that he lost his temper and snapped at his neighbour, 'What is this atrocity? How can they allow such hideous tortures to a helpless human being to be shown?' The spectator sitting next to him tried to hush him up. 'What's the matter with you?' he whispered at him. 'How long have you been here? Didn't you see what this man did before?' This is Joseph Mengele, the Nazi doctor of Auschwitz, who used inmates for human experiments, injecting chemicals into children's eyes and performing brutal surgeries and amputations on conscious people.

Likewise, when we choose to incarnate into a new lifetime in this world, we arrive in the middle of an endless movie displayed by the universe, so it is no wonder that life's events occasionally defy our understanding; no wonder that life baffles us. During times of painful crisis it is important to keep reaffirming over and over, that the universe works in perfect ways; that the law of cause and effect is constantly operating and whatever we are going through, whether it makes sense or not, is happening for a reason. Every stressful situation is an opportunity to pay karmic debts and heal old traumas by developing a loving acceptance for what is happening here and now. Zeno, the pupil of Socrates and founder of the Stoic school of philosophy, commanded, 'Love everything that happens to you.' Whether you view it as good or bad, it is happening with the purpose of leading you to your higher good.

We need to realise, though, that what we perceive as good or bad is our own biased judgement. What in life is good or bad? We love stuff that is terribly bad for us. We smoke, drink and do drugs that kill us prematurely despite strict medical warnings. We run a mile from things that are amazingly good for us. Usually we cannot imagine how a painful experience which we view as a bane can eventually turn out to be a boon.

The following old Indian story illustrates this. In a remote village, an old man and his son used their horse to cultivate a field. One day the horse ran away. The neighbouring villagers came over to visit the old farmer and sympathised, muttering, 'What a bad luck, what a bad break.' The old man said, 'Bad luck, good luck, who knows what's good or bad?' A week later the horse came back with five mares. The villagers came again and this time said, 'What good luck, what a fortunate break.' The old man said again, 'Good luck, bad luck, who knows what's good or bad?' A few days later, as his son was trying to tame one of the mares, he was forcefully kicked and broke his leg which then had to be put in cast. The old man kept saying, 'Good luck, bad luck, who knows what's good or bad?' A week later war broke out and the government people came to mobilise the young men of the village, but could not draft the old man's son, whose leg was in plaster. Good luck, bad luck, who knows what's good or bad? And the moral: Keep cool. A bad day is a good day in disguise.

Everything in life is designed for our higher good, including what we perceive as misfortunes, failures and setbacks. In times of crisis it helps to remind ourselves that life is unfolding perfectly, just like the music in a classical symphony. And we must trust the higher conductor to lead us to divine harmony, to enlightenment. It is only when we hate our hardships and resist the flow of life that it becomes hurtful. 'What you resist you persist,' says Dr Deepak Chopra. Everything that happens has been programmed for our unique spiritual needs; every eventuality is a custom-made opportunity to grow stronger, wiser and more loving; every human interaction gives us a chance to discard lower emotions.

To help do that, the Sufis have developed a 'turning

meditation'. In this mystic Islamic cult a practitioner visualises himself as an onion, and as he turns around pivoting on one leg, he imagines layers of the onion peeling off one by one, symbolising the shedding of his ego's lower emotions. The Sufis strive to arrive mentally at the core of the onion, at the emptiness of the bulb, which for them symbolises divinity. Emptiness, though, is not void. Emptiness is the potential source of all creative energy. In *The Holographic Universe*, Michael Talbot reports, 'When physicists calculate the minimum amount of energy a wave [field] can possess, they find that every cubic centimetre of empty space contains more energy than the total energy of all matter in the known universe.' Before the Big Bang there was nothingness and after a fraction of a second there was a whole universe. This is evident proof that what we call 'nothing' is indeed the source of everything, the root of all creation. Emptiness is the birthplace of fulfilment.

In times of crisis, the trick is to keep the faith, which, admittedly, is not easy. But holding even barely to the notion that in some mysterious way this hardship has a positive purpose helps lessen the emotional distress.

To make the law of cause and effect work for you, embrace the Taoist principle of 'attracting the positive with positive.' Strive to live your life with utmost integrity and kindness. Make it your highest priority to improve karma by creating positive causes that bring positive effects.

4

The Law of Attraction

Why are some people more successful than others? Why are some people living comfortably while others are struggling to make ends meet? Why do some people attract successes while others attract failures? Are some people naturally inclined to attract prosperity while others are less attractive?

The truth is that we are all very attractive. Within each one of us there is a powerful core of magnetic energy, a fragment of the universal creation power which is part of our divine identity. Each one of us is a walking electromagnet. Our brains and hearts are activated by electrical impulses which can be recorded on graphs by EEG and ECG machines. And just as a lump of iron induced with an electric current becomes a magnet, so do we human beings become magnetic by filling our minds with thoughts and emotions. Every time we use our mind we attract. And since our minds never stop thinking, we never stop magnetising and attracting. Our attraction power is constantly turned on. It is, however, an absolute power. It does not attract a little bit of this or a little more of that. It attracts without distinction whatever we think about. We can use it either way we want, constructively or destructively. Just as nuclear energy can be used to build either a weapon of mass destruction or a power station, so can we choose our attraction energy to work either for us or against us.

The law of attraction governs every aspect of our lives. It derives from the law of cause and effect. Just as each action attracts a corresponding reaction, so do our thoughts, feelings, emotions, beliefs and concepts, as spiritual causes, attract to us matching physical manifestations in the form of people, things and situations as effects. As such, we are constantly shaping our lives by the quality of our ideas, intents, opinions and aspirations.

Everything in this world—people, plants and minerals, as well as thoughts and feelings—has a unique vibration. Everything—you, me, the chair you're sitting on and the neighbour's lawn—transmits a vibrating energy of a specific wavelength. This vibration is an expression of spiritual energy, the creative energy of the universe from which everything is created. The only difference between various life forms or entities is that each has its own unique vibration. That is why our thoughts which determine our own vibration attract physical manifestations of identical vibration.

Just as a radio receiver can only receive a transmission on the same frequency as the broadcasting station, so we humans can only attract people and circumstances into our lives which match the vibration of our specific thoughts. Positive thoughts such as love and joy are of higher vibrations, whereas negative ones like hate and fear are of lower vibrations. But contrary to what many people believe, we are not slaves to our thoughts. We are indeed in control. We can choose what thoughts to think. We have the freedom of choice to choose higher or lower thought patterns. We can thus attract desirable or undesirable outcomes depending on the vibration emitted by our notions, ideas and aspirations.

The main reason there is so much pain, misfortune and failure in this world is because many people who lack self-love use the law of attraction in reverse. When you lie to someone, you are attracting people who will lie to you. When you are unfair to another, you are unfair to yourself because that is how others will treat you. When you con someone and think you have got away with it, think again. You are attracting the same low-vibration energy which will haunt you until the two actions are balanced out. Consequently, the initial requirement for a beneficial use of the law of attraction is constant purification of thoughts and actions. Striving to a higher level of love, compassion and morality is a sure way to improve our positive attractions.

Sometimes, however, we can be overwhelmed out of the blue by a challenging situation, an extreme experience or a personal crisis that defies our understanding. We may feel let down by the 'unfairness' of the issue because no matter how hard we think, we fail to see the relevance to our life of what is happening. That is because the law of attraction works both on a conscious level and on an unconscious level, a level we are not aware of. On this unconscious level, which is our part of divine wisdom, we attract people and situations which we need as lessons in order to learn and evolve. It is only in hindsight that we can realise that what we first interpreted as a regrettable misfortune actually presented us with higher understanding and new opportunities.

Becoming conscious of the fact that we attract all our experiences is a major milestone in our spiritual journey because we can then begin to accept responsibility for everything. We come to realise how futile it is to resent or blame people, fate or conditions for our predicaments. We finally realise that our present conditions are simply what we have magnetised by our previous thinking, feelings and intentions. And the good news is that from now on we can decide to attract only favourable desires and thus change our lives for the better.

To increase our attractive power we have first to be

convinced of its existence. We have to realise that we were born with this magnetism. We do not have to do anything to earn it. We are all endowed with this divine power as our birthright by a loving creator, who shares His power with us. We have to recognise it as part of our being. It is easier to start first by trusting the physical law that 'like attracts like'.

If you have two violins and play a note on one string, the corresponding string on the other violin will also vibrate. This is known in science as 'The Law of Sympathetic Resonance'. It means that two objects on the same frequency transmit energy to each other. Like the law of gravity, the law of attraction is absolute and consistent. It continuously attracts anything of the same vibration that you feed it. People affect each other in the same way. As human beings we are each a complex system of electromagnetic radiation, and when we feel attracted or in tune with another person, we are in fact flowing magnetic energy of the same wavelength—that is, of the same vibration.

But as magnetic beings that can easily attract prosperity and success, why do so many of us keep striving and struggling just to make ends meet? Why isn't everyone enjoying a brilliant life? It all stems from the basic teachings of our culture that extol the virtues of hard work to achieve anything. 'No pain no gain' has been accepted as part of our mentality which is based on the ego's limiting concept of scarcity. This is at the root of the common belief that to become rich you have to be dishonest and that having more money than you need is immoral. And that is why highly successful individuals are usually regarded with suspicion and resentment.

Although the law of attraction is very simple, it is not easy to practise. This is because, unfortunately, as a whole we tend to think practically—that is, pessimistically—on any life issue, personal or public. Suppose you were mistreated by a rival or even a lover. All too often we concentrate on the problem. We imagine mental pessimistic scenarios which drag us down to lower vibration thoughts. How come people dare to be so ungrateful? How to get even? How do we protect ourselves from recurring experiences? Such are some of the low-vibration thoughts we focus on and, sadly, those are the kind of experiences we attract. That is how we perpetuate and exacerbate the situation. That is how we use the power of attraction against us.

To boost our attractive power we must first realise that everything in this world is made up of non-physical, spiritual energy, the energy of all creation. To attract efficiently, just as radio receivers are tuned to the same frequency of the broadcast, we must attune ourselves to the energy broadcast of whatever we want. Whether it is money, a house, a car, a loving relationship or peace of mind, we must tune our minds to our specific goal in its spiritual form. It is as if we mentally 'merge' with the spiritual form of whatever entity we desire. We thus 'draw' it from the non-physical realm to its physical manifestation.

Although the law of attraction is straightforward, getting used to applying it properly takes time. We have to train our mind to accept the idea that whatever we want already exists in a spiritual form—just as we acknowledge the fact that there are countless radio transmission frequencies which are hidden and unavailable to us unless we tune to one specific frequency.

The greatest pitfall in attracting what we want is that our minds, through years of glorifying logic as the ultimate wisdom, try to analyse situations and problems rationally, to find logical solutions, and if none can be found, despair of the predicament, and resort to mentally visualising negative scenarios. It is amazing how most of us spend so much time contemplating on what we do not want. We are unwittingly flowing out low-vibration energy which is attracting the opposite of what we really want and then we complain that life works against us.

What you constantly think about, you attract. Whatever you habitually talk about, you draw to yourself. Words are fraught with emotion. Words can make you laugh, cry or blush in embarrassment. Words and thoughts engender feelings, sensations and mental pictures of the final outcome of whatever it is we have in mind, whether it is constructive or destructive. When you contemplate a Caribbean holiday in every enjoyable detail, or talk about buying a new classy car, you automatically feel excited and happy. When you keep blaming yourself for a blunder which you believe is your fault or keep talking about being betrayed by a friend, you feel bad. But these are exactly the kind of experiences that you attract in return for your thoughts and words.

Feelings are the greatest boosters of attraction. To energise your attraction you must feel passionate about your goal. You must feel excited. Your whole heart must be in getting what you want or it is pointless to go on. To boost your attractive energy and get things quicker, you must fire your heart with your enthusiasm, just as a blacksmith flares up a flame by pumping his bellows. You must feel the joy of achievement in your heart. To mentally see a goal as accomplished, to feel the buzz of having it, is the ultimate expression of faith power, a power that can create miracles. Strong feelings are extremely powerful. They amplify magnetism. They intensify attraction. Your feelings are the power of attraction in action. *You attract your desire by feeling as if you already got what you want now.* Feel the excitement of moving into your ideal house! Feel the pride of driving the car of your dreams! Feel the thrill of getting an unexpected bonus cheque from work!

Imagine a little boy brought by his dad to a huge toy store and told he could have anything he wants. Why, this boy will not be able to contain his excitement. He will be jumping up and down for joy. He will run in ecstasy through the aisles to pick up the PlayStation, the scooter, and the roller skates he always dreamed about. The truth is, our world is one gigantic toy store and as a child of God you can help yourself to whatever you intensely want and passionately desire. Your own ecstasy will attract it to you. Is it a pay rise, a soul mate, a college degree, a new house or a private plane? All is available if you can bring yourself to believe in your absolute right to have it.

Because we are constantly thinking, we are unaware that it is happening. Thoughts seem to come and go randomly. To attract positively, to magnetise only our cherished goals, we have to be vigilant about what goes on in our mind. Since thoughts create our reality, we must remind ourselves that negative thoughts are our enemies as they attract their equivalent expressions. When we have an inner ambition for a daring goal which seems beyond the ability of our rational mind to figure out, such as a new house when we already have two mortgages, or pursuing what seems a hopeless relationship with a heart-throb sweetheart, it is natural at first to feel our ego's doubts. Thoughts like 'Who do I think I'm kidding?' or 'Let's be realistic' tend to muffle our initial excitement. When you catch yourself thinking negatively, playing the role of a Doubting Thomas, or visualising an undesirable outcome, stop immediately. You are cutting the branch you are sitting on. Remind yourself that your thoughts are shaping your life and your concepts are creating your experiences. Realise that you are attracting the opposite of what you really want. You are playing the losing game. You are betraying your best interests. As Shakespeare put it, 'Our doubts are traitors/And make us lose the good we oft might win/By fearing the attempt.'

When we start thinking about something we emit a specific vibration. We set in motion minute particles of thought energy. When we keep thinking about it today, ponder over it tomorrow, reflect on it the next day and so on, we are weaving an energy pattern. Soon enough, these thought particles start clumping together to form bigger energy clusters, and if we keep focusing on our desire, these clusters keep growing until they become big lumps of huge vortexes of magnetic power. (At a certain point we will gradually start having a subtle feeling of this energy flow.) When these lumps reach a point of critical mass, they will act like a powerful eddy which will draw to it anything and everything of similar vibration. It will create a set of events which will culminate in actualising your final goal or send you inner guidance in the form of ideas, insights or urges to do something or go somewhere, which you should follow unquestionably. In hindsight, you will see that the things you were called upon to do formed a logical line of events, all leading up to your final goal which you initiated with your thinking.

The best way to attract any worthwhile goal is to let go and 'go with the flow'. Once you clearly know what you want, just do your energy work. Keep visualising it, anticipating it and feeling excited about it, but leave it at that. Do not try to make a deliberate effort of any kind to 'help' it happen in your own schedule. All you need do is patiently follow the unfolding chain of events as they occur, trusting that they are taking you there. The river of life may sometimes take a winding course toward your goal. Keep your cool even if it may seem as if it is taking you in a totally different direction altogether. In the long term it is a more effortless and harmonious way to attract your goal than struggling and striving. If nothing happens straight away, this is your test. The Higher Will may be testing you to see how much you believe in your goal. Pass the test victoriously. Continue to believe, for when you have passed one test you do not have a similar test to get through again.

Going with the flow should feel enjoyable, as if experiencing a fascinating adventure through a winding course, which is ultimately guaranteed to lead you to a happy end. Enjoy whatever scenery you encounter along the way and if something more appropriate and satisfying comes along, be flexible enough to accept it. The universe may be trying to show you a better alternative that you have not even considered. Throughout the experience, keep telling yourself that an unseen higher power is guiding you. Keep repeating to yourself to trust in a loving universe that works on your behalf, that wants to give you anything you desire as long as it is for your higher good, because it is true.

The law of attraction can be put to good use in various life issues. When you realise that like attracts like, you will never again stoop to criticise others or play the blaming game, because you do not want others to blame and criticise you. If you want to attract the good from other people, you will disregard their faults and concentrate on their higher traits. You will use only positive words and thoughts. In your speech, you will gradually train yourself to substitute positive words for negative ones. Instead of saying 'bad' you will say 'not good', and instead of 'hard' you will say 'not easy'. By optimising your thoughts and words you will be amazed at how much goodwill you will attract from other people, even from those you consider enemies. And as a bonus you will become proficient in diffusing tense situations. Remember that:

If you are courteous to others, others will be
courteous to you.
If you are patient with others, others will be patient
with you.
If you are sympathetic with others' plight, others will
be sympathetic with your plight.
If you are generous, others will be generous with you.
If you forgive others, others will forgive you.
If you love others, others will love you.

One of the greatest pitfalls in using the law of attraction favourably is our natural tendency to agonise over baffling problems or crisis situations. Our first automatic reaction is to focus on the problem, trying figure out ways to fix it. If we cannot find quick fixes, we become pessimistic and depressed. We tend to give up ever sorting out the situation. We indulge in imagining the worst possible scenarios. We complain to anyone who would listen. We put the blame on unfair people, dirty deals or adverse conditions beyond our control, not realising that at a certain level of thought it is us who attracted the problem in the first place. When we resent, complain and fret, we use the law of attraction to our detriment because the more we focus on our difficulty, the more we expand it and the deeper we sink.

The good news is that we can reverse the process. The law of attraction offers us an incredible opportunity to transcend troublesome problems by simply *refusing to dwell on them.* By switching our attention from the problem to the solution, we start to energise the law of attraction to work for us instead of against us. At first it may not be easy to untangle our minds from the distressing issues at hand and start feeling happy about a cherished something we do not have. Life-long habits have programmed us to be proactive, take the initiative and solve problems practically, rather than relying on some unseen power to work magic. But what if everything seems to conspire against you and no matter how hard you try, you don't see a way out? What if you lost your job, could not pay your mortgage and were threatened to be evicted? Instead of worrying and agonising about becoming homeless, turn your thoughts to happier scenarios. See yourself living happily in your house, relieved from financial worries, even if it looks totally absurd to your rationale. Trust the law of attraction to attract unexpected solutions and spontaneous opportunities to sort things out.

This is the time to realise that you do not need to strive

hard to change the situation, you just need to stop focusing on it. This is the time to realise that conditions really have no power over you. Reality is not as rigid as it may seem. It is pliable and can be shaped by your thoughts. Unpleasant reality is nothing more than the result of a negative energy flow. It is time to reprogramme your mind to rely more on your positive thoughts, feelings and intentions in order to create your cherished desires, rather than to depend on the finite wisdom of your conscious mind.

And use your new understanding to bless the crisis you are in, because it helps you clarify what you really want and leads you to a higher level of existence. Accept wholeheart-edly anything that life brings along. Feel grateful for your misfortunes. Feelings of acceptance and gratitude make you highly magnetic. Let go of the discomfort of being in disagreement with life. Agree with life, and life will agree with you. Once you learn to accept life, your condition will start to change for the better because you are now reaching to higher dimensions than the one you live in. Every moment you live in gratitude you connect with the higher power and once this gets to a high gear, magical things can happen. Remember, you can go through life accepting, approving, adoring, enjoying, or you can go through life constantly whining. Get rid of ingratitude and resentment and let magic flow.

Whether you want to be able to pay your bills, get financially comfortable or become wealthy, do not beg the universe for money. Do not wish you had money. Command money. Asking or wishing contain an element of uncertainty which frustrates your positive attraction, whereas an order is a powerful statement of assurance which stirs up excited feelings and visions of prosperity. And it is this excitement that you must feel each and every day which will eventually energise your attraction power and help attract what you want. Once you command money you must feel as thrilled as if someone told you that you have won the lottery. Do not think for a moment that you are being selfish or inconsiderate. It is your birthright to be sustained by a loving universe, just as trees and animals are provided for by the same cosmic power. You have the full right to claim your divine heritage, the size of which only you can decide. Through the law of attraction, life will always conspire to grant you anything you truly desire, barring nothing, provided you believe in your heart that you deserve it.

And have no qualms about the morality of becoming prosperous. Your success contributes to the success of others. Every dollar you put into circulation helps someone pay the rent and buy food for his family. The best thing you can possibly do for others, believe it or not, is to become successful yourself. Be careful though to want only what is good and right for you. Remember the famous saying, 'Beware of what you want, for you will get it.'

Choosing to focus on the higher qualities of people while ignoring their faults is a great way to use the law of attraction to improve relationships. This, however, may not come easy because, by nature, we always tend to analyse and criticise people and relationships in order to make us feel self-righteous. An unfaithful partner, an unruly youngster, a dishonest friend, an envious colleague, a mother-in-law from hell, or a rude supermarket cashier are some of our pet peeves which we particularly relish condemning. All too often we will rush to reprimand or chastise our offenders, trying to 'teach them a lesson'. We simply do not realise that our own resentful thoughts are emitting low-energy vibrations which attract and magnify the very flaws that vex us.

Giving up the need to dwell on others' shortcomings has several benefits. First of all we stop attracting more of the same. And as we stop playing the blaming game we obliterate the vicious cycle of condemning and forgiving. By visualising people *as if they have already changed for the better*, we influence their positive growth. We help them get attracted to their higher traits. We can gradually find that our higher vibration thoughts attract more peace of mind and better relationships.

If you want to be safe and secure, cultivate feelings of joy and confidence. Let the law of attraction use the flow of these high-vibration emotions to attract your own secured reality. Bad things happen to good people because they simply are not aware that the low vibrations of their fears, anxieties and worries are attracting the matching physical expressions of the same frequencies. Imagine two young girls walking in a dark alley late at night. One girl, who is feeling insecure and a bit panicky about the potential dangers lurking in this dire strait, hurries home. The other, feeling self-confident and fearless, walks tall and in high spirits, rehashing happy memories. Who do you think is more likely to get attacked? The answer is obvious. The insecure girl who is broadcasting low vibes of danger is more inclined to attract any evil-minded thug with corresponding vibes in the vicinity, whereas the confident, cheerful girl is more likely to attract some cheerful experience such as a lucky meeting with an old friend. The law of attraction works equally for anyone, young and old, men and women.

If you practise a cheerful and confident disposition, the law of attraction, properly used, can literally guarantee your safety. Start every day with a song in your heart. Be glad to be alive. And why is your positive mood so important? Simply because what you feel you vibrate, and what you vibrate you attract. As soon as a worry or a fear comes along, counter it with an optimistic statement. What do I do to beat the rare doldrums? I pick up my thesaurus and look up the word 'Happy'. It has a huge number of synonyms. By the time I finish reading all of them my mood is radically changed for the better. Every moment you live in happiness and confidence, nothing in this whole wide world can harm you. You are as safe as if you were covered by a divine shield. The degree of your safety from muggers, drunken drivers or freak accidents is in matching proportion to the level of your positive feelings of joy, love, gratitude and confidence. Conversely, worries and fears can only attract the very experiences you are anxious about.

When babies are born, do they arrive in this world with a long list of fears or worries? Do toddlers turn to one another and say things like, 'I'd love to play but I'm too stressed', 'I'm worried sick' or 'I'm not in the mood'? Tension, worry and stress are learned behaviours. We see the way other people behave and we copy them. To attract our own safe environment we have to unlearn these attitudes in order to get back to our natural state of well-being, ranging from basic contentment to ecstasy. To feel totally safe and secure we have to strive to upgrade our spiritual connection with life, to aspire to feel one with the power that created us, to return to the state of being in which our spirits exist, an ecstatic, blissful level of love and happiness.

5

Letting Go of Fear

Fear has been part of human consciousness for thousands of years and is still very prevalent on our planet. Its results can be seen globally in the form of aggression, conflicts and wars, and, on a more personal level, in duodenal ulcers, hypertension and heart attacks. It is important to realise that the feeling of fear is our heaviest burden. It ruins our peace of mind, kills our happiness and leads us to misguided, fear-based decisions.

Fear is the opposite of love. In fact, fear is usually caused by unloving attitudes of mind. Such thinking patterns tell you that the world is not a friendly place; that it is not loving and abundant; that it is a dog-eat-dog world; that people are out there to get you, and if you do not watch out you can be harmed. Sounds familiar? Of course. This is the voice of the ego which operates in terms of insecurity and scarcity.

Many people are so used to living in fear that they often do not even recognise it in themselves, since it becomes second nature. Fear can be disguised in those people who are extremely self-critical or low in self-esteem, who feel that they are not good enough, and who often find reasonable excuses not to proceed with daring projects and risk change. Such people will use all their rationale to come up with sensible, logical 'reasons' to explain both to themselves and to others why a new plan won't work.

How do you discover fear? Look for any unsatisfactory issue in your life which you would like to change but do not feel free to make a decision about. Typical fearful considerations are excuses such as you do not have enough money, you cannot make it on your own, people are not cooperating, you cannot bear the responsibility for the outcome or you may eventually fail so why try?

What is the solution? Start first by realising that this fear is an imaginary emotion which cannot restrict your life or bar you from fulfilling your deepest desires unless you allow it to. Take a few deep breaths and calm down. Silence your mind chatter for a minute. In a contemplative attitude connect mentally with your inner wisdom, your intuitive part which knows everything, past, present and future. Yes, everything. From a peaceful state of mind you can bring the higher wisdom of your unconscious mind into consciousness. Whether dumbfounded in a crisis situation or fearing to undertake a daring task, relax your mind and listen to any subtle, intuitive messages that come up. Be also aware of your physical feelings because your inner wisdom is often conveyed in body sensations. When you are considering an option or contemplating a course of action and get a feeling of an inner resistance, a heaviness or discomfort in the pit of your stomach, your body is warning you. This gut feeling is telling you that there is a better way to do it. But if you feel light and easy within, you will most likely hear something like, 'Go ahead,' or 'What you are most afraid of won't happen.' Take courage from it. Know that your body is an energy-sensing device. Trust the messages you receive.

It is important not to hate your fears or make them wrong because, after all, they are part of you. They came to protect you. Resisting your fears can only serve to intensify them. Instead, accept them and send them love and reassurance. Love helps to heal the lower emotions of fear by raising their vibration to a higher emotional level. Intense fear is a wake-up call. At the core of the most terrifying experiences lie the seeds of spiritual awakenings. When you reach a point where you feel fed up being scared and intimidated, fear can spark a journey of self-discovery. It is an opportunity to develop self-confidence by using affirmations or any empowering attitudes that can bolster your spirit.

Do not be afraid of those who act aggressively to impose their will on others. They often use anger to bully people and intimidate them in order to get their own way. Know that furious people are frightened people. They use anger as a defence mechanism, to compensate for their fears and disguise their own vulnerabilities. If someone attacks you or tries to wrong you, do not fear them or get into a temper. Instead, treat this person with compassion. Remember, the person who is trying to hurt you is your erring brother or sister, not an enemy. Compassion and love dissolve fear and help you grow; they offer you an opportunity to raise your consciousness to a higher vibration.

Control freaks are insecure people who live in constant fear of the future. So they try to prepare for every conceivable contingency. They forget that life is unpredictable. Some situations seek us no matter how hard we try to hide from them. In the words of Lau-Tsu, 'Life is a series of natural and spontaneous changes and resisting them only creates sorrow.' Control freaks often use their intellect to control the uncontrollable. They fabricate events, manipulate people and work hard to make things turn out in a certain way by pre-planning everything, down to the smallest detail. This is because they have not yet learned to surrender and trust life. They won't give life a chance because they will not muster the courage to flow in loving acceptance with whatever life brings. We all need to realise and constantly memorise that the power that created the problem at hand is the same power which, in its own perfect way, will provide the solution. To help overcome worry and anxiety, we must develop an intention to trust the wisdom of life.

Pursuing absolute security by shunning risks is senseless. As Helen Keller, the famous American deaf and blind inspirational lecturer, said, 'Security is mostly a superstition. It does not exist in nature, nor do the children of man as a whole experience it. Avoiding danger is no safer in the long run than outright exposure. Life is either a daring adventure, or nothing.'

It takes a lot of energy to make the world work in the way you think it should work. Put down this huge burden. Do not delude yourself that you are in control of every twist and turn in your life. Remember the last time an unexpected incident, seemingly coming out of the blue, took you by surprise. Indeed you *are* in charge of your destiny, you are the captain of your fate, but only to the extent of setting the goals you desire. By setting specific goals, you enlist the power within and give direction to your divine creativity, which will go out and organise events that will manifest them for you in the perfect way and in the perfect time. All you need to do is to be attentive to your gut feelings and act on them. It is easier to dissipate fear when you convince yourself that you are a channel of an unlimited inner power.

Love is a great fear healer. The healing energy of love can actually help cure specific irrational fears such as phobias. Suppose you are afraid to walk in the dark, ride an elevator or board a plane. Try to do these things anyway, and while doing them, send a strong surge of love deep down to the fear within. When you love your fear you provide it with reassurance. If you do this sincerely, you may feel that the fear is greatly alleviated. The dark shadows of fear, worry and anxiety cannot be pushed away physically. They can be removed not by resistance or will power but by illuminating them with the light of love.

In daunting situations it is very tempting to run away from the cause of trouble. This is counterproductive. Fearful challenges have a constructive role to play. They are intended to make you stronger and more confident in a particular aspect of your life. By avoiding them you avoid the lesson. Only by facing fear can you overcome it. As Ralph Waldo Emerson said, 'Do the thing you fear and death of fear is certain.'

The importance of facing our fears is illustrated by an event reported by the American Buddhist nun Pema Chödrön in her book *When Things Fall Apart*. In it she relates the story of her Tibetan teacher who once led a group of children to visit a monastery. A ferocious, menacing dog was chained to the gate. A while later, as the group was near the entrance of the monastery, the dog suddenly broke free and started to run towards the kids. Everyone froze in terror. The teacher immediately turned around and started running towards the dog as fast as he could. Taken totally by surprise, the dog turned back and ran off.

All too often in life we let fear get the better of us. We waste hours, days and even weeks so caught up in our apprehensions that we can hardly think about anything else. As Helen Keller said, 'We often look so long at the closed door that we do not see the one which has been opened for us.' We are so focused on the cloud that we do not see the silver lining. Eventually the clouds clear and we see how silly we have been. We have spoiled our most valuable possession—our ability to enjoy life. We forget that an occasional knock is part of life, and it, too, has its beneficial role. Indeed, we all live in a world which was first dubbed by the American humorist George Ade in 1912 as the 'school of hard knocks', an idiomatic expression which refers to painful experiences that are meant to teach us about life.

A fleeting panic is a blessing. It offers a chance to face fear and conquer it by developing a tougher resolve and stronger confidence. This is how we bolster our spirit. Those of us who try to avoid fear by not taking risks are missing the point. Challenging situations are a natural part of life. Risks are gateways to opportunities. Actually, opportunities often come disguised as misfortunes or temporary defeats. If you are not willing to take chances, you will always play it safe. You will not undertake any risky ventures; you will not dare to pursue your heart's desires.

Spontaneous alarms serve beneficially as urgent warnings. In fact, abrupt fears are the reason mankind exists today. Throughout history, sudden frights in dangerous situations have triggered the 'fight or flight' reaction, the adrenalin rush which is responsible for the survival of humanity. Going through life nowadays still means encountering alarming experiences, dealing with them and then forgetting them. It is prolonged fears, however, that take their long-term toll on us. But these too can be a blessing in disguise. When we have decided that we had enough of their torture, that we cannot take them any longer, we can then enlist the courage to trust our power within and become fearless. Fear can make us more powerful only if we choose to face its cause and overcome it.

For any of us who are determined to evolve spiritually— that is, to grow stronger, happier and more loving—over-coming the torment of lifelong insecurity is the first challenge. As Thomas Carlyle said, 'The first duty of a man is that of subduing fear; he must get rid of fear; he cannot act at all till then, his acts are slavish, not true.' So work on your interconnectedness with life. Keep repeating, 'I am a child of God, offspring of universe, part of nature; I am larger than my experience; no matter what happens, the higher power that keeps me alive will lead me to handle it.' Believe it to be true, because it is.

The so-called fear of God is often used by people who want to manipulate or subdue others. Since God is everlasting love, why should anyone fear God? Personally, I would exchange 'awe' or 'reverence' for the word 'fear'. When the Bible says, 'Blessed is the man that feareth the Lord' (Psalms 112:2), it means: blessed is the man who fears the consequences of the law of cause and effect. If we act in a fearful, hostile or any unloving way that creates hurt, we have all the right to fear the law's forthcoming retribution. Anything we do comes back either to chastise us or to reward us. According to the Buddhist law of karma, there are no coincidences, only karmic incidents. It is our own choices that create our heaven or our private hell.

Sow a fear and reap an abuse. A specific fear is the cause which attracts a matching abuse as its effect. It is therefore pointless to blame the abuser. Remember how clearly the book of Job in the Bible expresses this? While lamenting his terrible fate, Job mourns: 'For the thing which I greatly feared is come upon me and that which I was afraid of is come into me' (Job 3:25). Of course. Job was actually confirming the law of cause and effect in action. Only he used it in reverse. In the first daunting days of World War II, when the American people were deeply terrified by what might lie in store, it was President Franklin Delano Roosevelt who raised the morale of his nation by proclaiming, 'The only thing we must fear is fear itself.'

Fear is an unpleasant sensation. The most common way to disguise it is through addictions. Alcohol and drugs distort our consciousness and suppress our emotions, allowing us a temporary escape from reality. They make us feel high or numb, unable to feel anything, and for a while we forget our troubles. In challenging situations, many people routinely take a drink or two to boost their mettle. Obviously, alcohol and drugs are not a cure for fear. They can only disguise it temporarily, and charge a high price in health and dependency.

We may sometimes be confronted with dismaying crisis situations, from unexpectedly losing a job to an impending financial catastrophe, and from apprehensions which cause a minor anxiety to panics that initially paralyse us. We each have a different threshold for fear. Some people meet their edge by having to speak in public or asking the boss for a raise, while others thrive in bungee jumping. There are no standard fear levels for comparison since we each have our own unique tolerances. Everyone has to meet his or her own personal demons and learn to overcome them. This takes courage. The courage of facing fears. But courage, contrary to what many people think, is not the absence of fear. Absence of fear is a mental anomaly. Courage is the ability to go ahead despite the fear. Just like the title of Susan Jeffers' successful book, *Feel the Fear and Do it Anyway*.

A few years ago I read a report about an English agora-phobe (someone who is morbidly fearful of open places). This man grew so desperate with his distressing condition that he decided to end his life. He drove his car for a couple of miles to the countryside, an experience so frightening that he felt sure it would kill him. When his plan did not work, he first felt shocked but then he was surprised to discover that his fear had greatly reduced.

Fear is born of separation. It arises from the feeling that you are alone in this world. That there is no one available for help when you find yourself in trouble. This is a very daunting feeling. It is also untrue. Such thinking patterns contravene your oneness with universal consciousness; such attitudes contradict your divine connectedness, your con-nection with God. Our souls are part of the divine. In the book of Proverbs, King Solomon said that the light of God is the soul of human being. We are each an individualised divinity.

Developing an awareness of oneness with the universe, or establishing a connection with God, is a powerful cure of fear. As you reflect on this divine–human connection, you magnify it. Get into the habit of talking to God regularly, as you would talk to your most intimate friend. Share with Him your insecurities, concerns and aspirations, then listen to your inner messages. Eventually you will develop an awareness of connectedness and will gradually experience a growing sense of peace and security. In time, you will come to realise that you are looked after by the same power of life that keeps trees growing, birds flying and rivers flowing. It is the higher power that sustains this universe. This power is always operating; it is constantly looking after you. It is the power that is with you through any adversity you may be faced with. As you develop an awareness of God as your constant companion, you are gradually dissolving your insecurities. When a sudden fright comes along, conceive of yourself as being surrounded by a golden light that embraces you. Imagine this light to be warm, loving and powerful, making you feel safer and stronger almost instantly. This is your soul. Know that you can call on this light whenever you feel vulnerable.

Our inner connection to the power within us is our spiritual grounding. It gives us staying power and endurance in periods of distress. Without it, we are like a tree devoid of roots; any casual gust can fell it. Intuitively, most of us feel a need for this unity, as deep inside we all have a subtle yearning to reconnect with our source. Short of it, we may feel that something is missing. Different people find it in different ways, such as religion, spiritual growth workshops, Buddhist gurus or mystic sects. Some are deluded into looking for it in dubious venues. This is why bizarre cults are on the rise.

In the Judaeo-Christian tradition the Bible repeatedly claims that fear can be cured by developing faith attitudes, by cultivating an awareness of God's loving presence and by actually establishing a mental connection with God. For example: 'Fear not ... for the Lord thy God, He is that goes with thee; He will never fail thee nor forsake thee' (Deuteronomy 31:6). If you keep repeating this or similar Bible affirmations over and over, you will gradually develop a confident awareness. Eventually, you will claim back your power.

Another common source of fear is falsehood and deceit. When you do not speak the truth, when you dishonestly manipulate your way to an egoistic purpose because of lack of self-confidence, you project fear: the fear of being found out. This makes you live in insecurity. You have to be constantly vigilant since you never know when through a spontaneous verbal slip, the karma of deception will come back to haunt you. Remember the saying, 'Nothing to hide, nothing to fear'. Truthfulness is the gateway to fearlessness.

At certain times, when we feel vulnerable or insecure, we may weave a tangled web as we set out to deceive in order to protect our privacy. When we are straightforward we seemingly have no cloth for protection. To be honest is to be naked and on a sunny day this may be glorious, particularly with other sympathetic sunbathers. But when it starts to rain and people are sniggering at our exposure, the desire to cover up grows. We need a source of heat to compensate for our vulnerability. This source of heat is our faith in life. We must let faith be our furnace.

We all have expectations and needs. Sometimes, when expectations such as financial needs are not immediately met, we may become insecure and resentful. We need to realise that life is mysterious. Life is full of uncertainties. Our journey may take us through some rough patches which are beyond explanation or understanding. Uncertainty,

69

however, is part of life. It is a gateway to a new range of possibilities. Do not hate it, welcome it. Expect to be amazed and keep an open mind. Instead of letting precarious situations scare you, better learn to accept them as part of life. Trust that they are perfectly happening for your higher good, and in one way or another, they are serving your spiritual evolution.

To help overcome fear-related stresses and anxieties, several powerful tools such as affirmations, meditation, prayer, body work or music can be used. You have to find one that suits you best. What all these methods have in common, though, is the ability to calm the mind and induce relaxation. And it is only when the body is relaxed and the mind is calm that the whispers of our inner wisdom can be heard. It is only in tranquillity that surprising ideas can pop up and problems become clarified, pointing a way out, a path through. A peaceful mind opens a channel to the divine wisdom within us.

Prayer is a great way to abate fear and boost confidence. By praying regularly, we connect with the power of all creation. By making non-formal prayers a way of life, we build a strong conviction which, in time, dissolves fears and insecurities. We gradually develop an inner 'knowing', a feeling that we are divinely guided and protected on a higher level. Prayer has also a soothing effect. It helps purge the mind from self-defeating thoughts and sets our concepts and views on a more positive track. And eventually, the practice of prayer causes our compassion and our self-love to evolve.

But doesn't God know everything already? Doesn't He know when we are in trouble and need His help? Why do we need to pray at all? A quotation from *Taming the Atom* by Hans Christian Von Baeyer illustrates this: 'The physicist Leo Szilard once announced to his friend Hans Bethe that he was thinking of keeping a diary: "I don't intend to publish. I am merely going to record the facts for the information of God." "Don't you think that God knows the facts?" Bethe asked. "Yes," said Szilard. "He knows the facts, but He does not know *this version of the facts.*"' Actually, prayer is not appealing to some distant deity. Prayer is an inner practice. It establishes a connection with our own spiritual self.

God is the oneness of all life. He does not need to be begged for help. In prayer we simply move to a place of a loving acceptance deep within us, opening our heart to trust in the sustaining power of life. Prayers are really a spiritual mind treatment. This is why we often feel a sense of relief after a deep emotional prayer. We have made a connection with our source of oneness.

Prayer does not even need words. A feeling is also a prayer. By concentrating on a feeling, a desire or an emotion, we are actually praying. We release a spiritual energy that vibrates with the power of all creation. Rather than making the world change, a feeling-based prayer changes us. As the nineteenth-century Danish philosopher Soren Kierkegaard said, 'Prayer does not change God, but it changes him who prays.' And as we change, so do our circumstances.

Prayers can be in the form of either supplications or affirmations. A supplication is a humble appeal to a higher power seemingly outside us, such as, 'Please help me God.' Affirmations, on the other hand, are in the form of factual statements. They affirm, or 'make firm', our oneness with the divine power. For example, 'The Lord is the strength of my life' (Psalms 27:1). Both forms can be beneficial when done with deep conviction. Affirmations, however, can be more empowering to the spirit. By permeating the unconscious mind they act like a hypnotic suggestion. Prayers deepen our faith by linking us to our souls.

Faith is what makes prayers work. 'What things so ever

you desire, when you pray, believe that you receive them and you shall have them' (Mark 11:24). Any kind of prayer must be backed by an inner certitude in its outcome, by a strong belief that it is being answered. Faith means accepting as true even what reason and logic deny. You develop faith by constantly refusing to listen to your fearful and doubtful thoughts which hold you back, and adopting instead an attitude of complete reliance on the goodness of the universe of which you are part. It is your trust in the goodness of God which supports life that will make you feel protected.

Fear negates faith. It arises from an underlying assumption that there may be a power opposed to God. It may not be easy to change lifelong habits of relying only on your doubtful thoughts, but relentlessly aspiring to develop a faithful reliance on the higher power which sustains life is one of the best gifts you can give yourself.

To pray efficiently, we need to pray in God's terms. God is love, peace, creativity and abundance. Fear, scarcity and turmoil are alien to God's nature. So instead of praying for something that is missing, such as money, love or health, we must pray in God's terms, as in the famous prayer of St. Francis, 'God, make me an instrument of your love,' or, 'God, make me a channel of your abundance.'

Affirmations are powerful statements that can help focus your awareness on your inner strength. They can thus increase power and decrease fear. Affirmations are always stated in the present tense, as if they were actual facts. They are worth repeating over and over, day in, day out, until their truth permeates the unconscious mind, the seat of our deeper awareness. The unconscious mind is non-judgemental; it accepts whatever statement you choose to make. Once the unconscious reprogrammes your affirmations as a reality, you become aware of your power. You begin to consciously think and act in a way that matches the newly conceived reality. Eventually, you will think and act from a higher, more powerful level.

We are each impacted differently by various affirmations, and for maximum effect, should choose the specific ones that resonate with us; the ones that 'click'. We can even create our own, as long as they are positive and phrased in the present tense. Following are two examples of powerful affirmations that can help substitute fear with strength. Choose one or both on different occasions. To saturate the mind with their essence, they are best repeated several times daily:

- I believe I am always divinely guided.
- I believe that I shall always take the right turn of the road.
- I believe that God will always make way where there is no way.

- The light of God surrounds me,
- The love of God enfolds me,
- The power of God protects me,
- The presence of God is watching over me,
- Wherever I am, God is.

Affirmations focus your attention on your strength. As a result, fear is ignored and withers away. In *How to Cultivate Confidence and Promote Personality*, psychologist Dr Gilbert Oakley writes, 'I fear nothing. Least of all I fear being afraid. I know there is no such thing as fear. I know there is a reasonable sense of precaution, care and commonsense. I see everything in its correct perspective and right proportion. This being so, I have no need for fear.'

Fear is lack of trust in our link with universal life. We become fearful when we do not trust our connection with the power of all creation, when we forget that each one of us contains the divine spark. We are each Spirit individualised.

We can regain our innate courage when we constantly remind ourselves that our bodies are the temples of our souls and that deep within, we are each a focus of the universal creation which is there to protect us. Our inner intuition is an early warning system whose main job is to safeguard life. All we need do is listen to its premonitions and trust them. Once you have taken all necessary steps to deal with a crisis situation, relax. When destiny forces your hand, go with the flow. Adopt a calm, open-minded attitude and when you get an inner impulse or a subtle whisper to do something, act on it.

To act on what you hear you have to take the leap of faith. When you get a strong urge to take a certain action, believe that this is the voice of your higher self guiding you. If an inner impulse is urging you to go out and do something which seems totally senseless, do it anyway, even if you question your sanity while doing it.

This takes courage. But it helps to remember that the only thing greater than the power of the mind is the courage of the heart. Think back on a previous personal crisis, a time when you were in serious trouble, when you were totally at a loss, when suddenly, an unexpected event or an amazing coincidence made a way for you where before there was no way. Many people can recall such lucky breaks. Some can even remember astonishing incidents when a strange urge to miss a train, change a flight or give up a car ride actually saved them from a fatal accident. Rehashing such unexplainable incidents can help make you aware of your guardian angel who is always looking after you. Reminiscing on such events can help you gradually to realise that you are constantly protected in whatever situation you find yourself in. It is only when you get to actually sense the presence of a protective intelligence around you that you can feel safe. You then know that you have no need for fear.

Life is risky. It has always been full of threats. In the

sixties, it was the nuclear arms race of the cold war, when we expected the world to end. In the seventies, population experts predicted that we would all be starving and fighting for space. In the eighties, AIDS threatened to decimate the world's population. In the nineties, we discovered global warming and we started to shiver! So far, despite all this, most of us are still here. The threats are still real . . . but so too is hope. Now, allowing for this natural tendency to expect the sky to fall at any moment . . . just how valid is your current personal fear?

In his book *Zen Showed me the Way*, actor Sessue Hayakawa, who played Colonel Saito in *The Bridge on the River Kwai*, tells the following story: 'Some years ago, a European college professor visiting in Japan was talking with some Japanese on the fifth floor of a hotel in Tokyo. Suddenly they all heard a rumbling. "There was a gentle heaving under our feet," the European later noted. The swaying and creaking and the crash of objects became more and more pronounced. Alarm and excitement mounted. The terror was all the greater because the great Japanese earthquake of 1923 was still fresh in memory. People rushed out of the room into the corridor to the stairs. Professor Eugene Herrigel, the European professor, asked the Japanese gentleman with whom he had been talking why he did not hurry to run for safety. "I noticed to my astonishment," Professor Herrigel said, "that he was sitting there unmoved, hands folded, eyes nearly closed, as though none of it concerned him". . . . The Japanese who remained so unperturbed was a Zen Buddhist. He had put himself into a state of extreme concentration and thus became unassailable.'

It seems almost incredible that after so many devastating wars in recent history, humanity is still plagued with the fear of international terrorism which glorifies the culture of suicidal death. Terror has created global uncertainty. Chemical and biological weapons of mass destruction against civilian populations are threatening our very existence. In these times, no less than ever before, we each need to do our utmost to overcome fear. Like the Zen Buddhist, we can strive to become unassailable by keeping constantly aware of the power within and by concentrating our attention on our inner connectedness with the higher Presence that lovingly sustains us.

6

Love and Prosper

As we transcend the limiting boundaries of the ego, with its fears and scarcity programming, and cross over into self-love, we start to realise that love is the key to real prosperity. When you love yourself enough, you will naturally want to enjoy life more. You will desire the highest and the best. You will aspire to flourish. The power of all creation is infinite. The universe is a place of endless abundance and prosperity. And as you are part of it, prosperity is your birthright. Abundance is your legacy. All you need to do is to claim it. 'Ask, and it shall be given you' (Matthew 7:7).

The universe is dynamic, not static. It has been expanding since the Big Bang as old galaxies collapse and new ones spread out at great speeds. The natural tendency of life is to procreate and multiply, reproducing itself in ever-increasing affluence. Similarly, the abundance of our own planet earth is constantly multiplying. Just compare the living standards of average people today with those of bygone centuries. Where a few decades ago major companies had annual turnovers of millions, their turnovers are now in the billions. More people are becoming millionaires. When once most of the population had to toil in the fields all day long for a meagre existence, nowadays in western countries less than five per cent do, many in air-conditioned tractors. People starve today in poor countries not because of lack, but because of uneven distribution of the world's resources.

When you prosper, do not feel guilty; you are not depriving anyone. There is more than enough for all of us. Gandhi said, 'There is enough in this world for everyone's need, but not enough for everyone's greed.'

Human beings reflect the abundance of the universe as microcosms. Each human body is made up of a staggering 60 to 80 trillion cells, or about 10,000 times the world's population. And just like the universe, the human body is constantly changing. Ninety eight per cent of the atoms in our bodies change every year. That means that we are renewing ourselves annually. We get a new skin every month and new blood cells every three months. Our bodies are not afraid to lose cells because abundant new supplies keep being created.

All this infinite abundance is the manifestation of divine consciousness, which is constant creativity. Divine consciousness has also an infinite capability. It holds a potential of countless possibilities, endless probabilities. It has limitless organising powers of events, far beyond our understanding. It has the ability to express itself magically, in anything and everything, and in unlimited amounts. And being part of the same divine intelligence, we have the same infinite creative potential for prosperity. Once we realise that our own human consciousness is part of divine consciousness, it is obvious that the place to create prosperity and abundance is not out there somewhere, but inside our own consciousness.

Divine abundance is available for the asking. It is available to all those who are aware of their birthright to claim it. The size of your consciousness determines the size of your bank account. Imagine that infinite abundance is an endless ocean to which people come to draw water. Some come with a cup, others with a bucket, while others dare to come with a power hose. Your share of this infinite abundance depends directly on how big your claim is. The ocean does not question the size of your container. If you want more you simply have to change your belief system about what you deserve. You just need to change your mental programming from *scarcity programming* to *prosperity programming.*

Prosperity is a state of mind that manifests itself in every area of living, not just wealth, but also health, happiness and loving relationships. To prosper means to be fortunate or successful, to thrive. When you are prosperous, you feel that you flow with life. You feel that life is working for you, not against you.

Since it is our consciousness that creates our reality, it behoves us to develop a consciousness of prosperity. Think prosperity, speak prosperity. Start by expanding your thinking patterns. Mentally allow yourself to have more. Open yourself to receive. Imagine that all the abundance of the universe is already self-contained in your consciousness. You only have to draw it out. Just as a seed planted in the soil attracts to itself everything it needs to sprout and grow, so can we plant a seed-thought of a desire in our mind, faithfully expecting it to draw to itself all the means for its accomplishment. Eliminate, therefore, old thoughts of lack. Believe that everything is possible. Realise that the thoughts that you entertain are creating your world. Decide as a result to dismiss the doubtful thoughts that say that you cannot have what you want. Forget about doom and gloom news. Forget about recessions because there are those businesses which thrive even during recessions. 'A man's life is what his thoughts make of it,' said the Roman emperor and sage Marcus Aurelius. Thoughts are energy; they possess dynamic power. When you think about a goal, you give direction to the power of all creation within you. You become a co-creator with God.

If prosperity is a state of mind, so is poverty. Anthony Santangelo came to the United States from Italy after he heard that America is the land of opportunity. He firmly believed that anyone can get rich in America. With his wife Maria, he bought a hamburger stand at the front of a little farm and started to make hamburgers. Their hamburgers were delicious and their stall prospered. They worked long hours but they did not mind; they loved it. Gradually they added more items like homemade bread and pastries. Their business grew by word of mouth and people would travel distances to eat at Tony's place. Eventually, the stall grew into a diner. They hired an extra cook for the kitchen and a gardener to grow fresh vegetables. They were even planning a small gift shop on the side. By now, they could afford to send Tony Jr. to college. They also started making plans for a new and larger house to replace the little cottage they lived in. Their future looked very promising. They were successful, just as they thought they would be before they came to America.

When Tony Jr. came home for his Christmas holiday, they could not wait to show him the plans. Tony Jr. was shocked, but for the wrong reason. And this was the turning point. 'Haven't you heard about the coming depression?' he asked them. 'Times are not good now. Don't you read newspapers?' His parents confessed that they were so busy working that they did not have time to read newspapers. However, they took their son's ideas seriously. After all, wasn't he studying business management in college? He surely had to know, they thought. Maybe they had better prepare for a recession. So they started cutting back. They first cancelled their plans for a new house, which was a shock to the architect and the builder who, in return, also had to cut back their own staff. Then, since the recession was right around the corner, Tony and Maria reckoned, there would be no need for the gift shop, a decision which dismayed the salesgirl they had assigned to run it.

It was no longer much fun to eat at Tony's place. Customers did not like the sombre faces of Tony and his wife. Soon the couple had to let the cook go. The cook was a widow who had to support her little children, but what could she do? She just passed around the news that business was bad and the restaurant was failing. Now Tony and Maria felt they could do without the home-grown vegetables, so the gardener had to go, and he in turn told his friends how bad business was now. News travelled fast and fewer and fewer people were coming to Tony's place. At last, the depression seemed to be about to hit. Eventually, however, the news about the imminent depression turned out to be a false alarm which had been started as political propaganda. But by the time Tony found this out, he felt too tired and disheartened to start all over again. He learned too late to listen more to his prosperity thoughts and less to bad rumours. Tony prospered as long as he believed he could prosper and failed when he did not believe he could prosper. When he lost his faith he used the laws of prosperity in reverse.

The laws of the universe also govern prosperity. The law of attraction, as explained in Chapter 4, means that whatever you think or expect, you draw to yourself. This law is impartial, so you can use it to attract prosperity, poverty or just a mere subsistence. Fortunately, we were given the gift of free choice. So choose to think in an optimistic way. Don't listen to doom and gloom mongers because life is an individual experience. Your life is what you yourself make of it. When pessimistic thoughts come up, discard them immediately. They are your enemies. Substitute negative thoughts with positive ones. Be discriminating with your thoughts. Select them carefully. You cannot afford the luxury of negative thinking.

If you cannot perceive that thoughts and expectations can make things happen, you may be comforted to know that this idea was also puzzling the best scientific minds. Since the early 1900s, the world's leading physicists have been baffled by strange behaviour of electrons and other sub-atomic particles. Electrons sometimes behaved like particles and sometimes like waves; an electron could disappear from one orbit and reappear in another without visiting the space between, in what became known as the famous 'quantum leap'. These mind-boggling oddities were finally resolved in 1926 by the German physicist Werner Heisenberg in his 'Quantum Mechanics', a discipline which highlighted the Uncertainty Principle. Accordingly, an electron or a photon of light can be either a particle or a wave, *depending on how you regard it and expect it to be.* Similarly, you create any experience you imagine. You can actually choose your own reality! The power of visualisation and expectation to make things happen was eventually proven as a property of the universe.

Our minds live in a quantum field. Thoughts are electro-magnetic impulses of information which strongly attract their physical manifestations. Thoughts can be conveyed telepathically not only to humans; the energy of thought pervades everything, living or non-living. In the famous philodendron experiment, when the CIA lie-detector expert Cleve Backster wired his plant to a polygraph and held the thought, 'I'm going to light a match and burn the stem,' the polygraph needle started to flicker frantically. It showed that even plants can sense thought energy.

In *Creative Mind and Success* Dr Ernest Holmes, originator of the 'Science of Mind' and founder of the Religious Science Movement, gives a beautiful description of mind over matter. He writes, 'Just imagine yourself surrounded by Mind, so plastic, so receptive, that it receives the slightest impression of your thought. Whatever you think, it takes up and executes for you. Every thought is received and acted upon. Not some, but all thoughts. Whatever the pattern we provide, that will be our demonstration. If we cannot get over thinking we are poor, then we will remain poor. As soon as we become rich in our thought, then we will be rich in our expression. These are not mere words, but the deepest truth that has ever come to the human race. In the centre of your own soul choose what you want to become, to accomplish; then keep it to yourself. Every day in the silence of absolute conviction know that it is done. For it is just as much done, as far as you are concerned, as it will be when you experience it in the outer. Imagine yourself to be what you want to be. See only that which you desire, refuse even to think of the other. Stick to it, never doubt. Say many times a day, "I am that thing" and realise what this means. For it means that the great universal power of Mind is that, and it cannot fail.'

It is vitally important to keep thinking positively, no matter what your situation, especially if you are going through a rough patch. The late Mike Todd used to say, 'I have been broke many times but I have never been poor.' Reframing the negative into the positive opens up creative channels. Successes or failures are merely states of mind. When you faithfully expect a goal, you activate the law of attraction. Excitement and passion release the greatest attraction energy. The more excited you are about it, the quicker it will be attracted to you. It is really sad that so many people are cynical about the generous nature of the universe. They do not believe that prosperity is their natural birthright. They mostly dwell on negative thoughts, such as how hard life is, how unfair things are. To succeed, you must think positively. Remember: If you keep thinking what you have always thought, you will be getting what you have always got.

Many people are underachievers because they have a concept of scarcity, as if life's resources are limited and may run out. They make bleak predictions about any undertaking, not realising that they are thus blocking the flow of creative energy. They are so afraid of being disappointed that they do not dare to assert themselves positively about any plan of action, should it not work out. They do not dare to take the leap of faith. They do not realise that by merely expecting a successful outcome, they are actually creating it.

In order to prosper you must open yourself up and allow the free-flowing abundance of the universe to flow into your life. Strange as it may seem, many people have difficulty accepting their own good. Such people simply lack self-love. As a result, they have a low sense of self-worth. They confuse accepting, receiving and prospering with greed. For them, it is morally better to give than to receive. They are not aware that we all equally share life's riches. Allowing the gifts of the universe is of primary importance. Prosperous people are good receivers. They have learned to accept their good as their natural birthright, without any guilt feelings. In *Living Without Gloves*, Halford E. Luccock writes: 'It is more blessed to give than to receive. But the givers who cannot take in return miss one of the finest graces in life, the grace of receiving. To receive gratefully from others is to enhance others' sense of their worth. It puts them on a give-and-take level, the only level on which real fellowship can be sustained. It changes one of the ugliest things in the world, patronage, into one of the richest things in the world, friendship.'

On the road to the fulfilment of your desires you will occasionally encounter various opportunities, and you must be open to accept them as they come. The word *opportunity* is derived from the Latin term, *ob portu*, or to-port, when ships had to wait for the high tide to bring them into the harbour. Once they missed it, they had to wait for the next tide. Likewise in life, when an opportunity presents itself, you must be ready to take it. Shakespeare beautifully highlighted this issue in *Julius Caesar*, Act 4, Scene 3:

There is a tide in the affairs of men,
Which, taken at the flood, leads on to fortune;
Omitted, all the voyage of their life
Is bound in shallows and in miseries.
On such a full sea are we now afloat;
And we must take the current when it serves,
Or lose our ventures.

Whatever you think about, increases in your life. Whatever you contemplate is energised. Whatever you identify with, you become. When you say with full and sincere conviction, 'I am prosperous,' you already are. So focus on your strengths. Refuse to think about your weaknesses. By thinking, acknowledging and blessing your prosperity, you create a consciousness of prosperity. You invoke the law of increase. You begin to see abundance where others see scarcity. To change your thinking patterns, it is very useful to repeat positive affirmations over and over until they get hold of your consciousness. Until they become part of your belief system. Following are some examples of such affirmations, from which you can choose the ones that impact you the most:

- Life is abundant. I see abundance everywhere.
- All of life is now working with me to bring about my prosperity.
- I am one with universal abundance.
- The power of all creation is within me.
- Prosperity is the law of my life.
- As a child of God, I now claim my divine heritage.
- New opportunities open up to me just as I need them.
- Life's infinite riches are now freely flowing into my life.
- I now materialise my unlimited potential.

In *Positive Magic*, author Marion Weinstein describes a category of affirmative statements called *words of power*. Adopted from the school of positive occult, or white magic, these words are phrased in an affirmation format designed to help create any positive goal. To illustrate, let's use this statement for the goal of *fulfilment*:

There is one Power.
And this Power is perfect fulfilment.
And I (your name) am a perfect manifestation of this
    Power.
Therefore, perfect fulfilment is mine, here and now.
For the good of all,
According to the free will of all,
And so it must be.

To create any goal, you simply substitute the word 'fulfil-ment' with anything you wish, such as abundance, prosper-ity, love or happiness.

To become more prosperous you have to believe that everything is possible. You must learn to accept miracles as a way of life. When you believe in the marvellous you can start gradually sensing the subtle feeling of a higher wisdom working in your life. It is easier to believe in miracles when you realise that the universe has an infinite organising power which can create incredible events, far beyond your ability to comprehend. Many people, however, are more sceptical about miracles. They call them coincidences, flukes, windfalls or events that happened out of the blue. Some think that miracles are a biblical phenomenon. The fact is, however, that miracles happen all the time. Miracles are part of our daily lives. But lots of these gifts are wasted because most people are too blind to see them as heavenly presents. When you become more aware of the miraculous occurrences in your life, when you recognise any unexpected opportunity or event as a miracle and thank the universe for it, you attract more of the same into your life. You become luckier and more successful. As Albert Einstein remarked, 'There are only two ways to live your life. One is as though nothing is a miracle. The other is as if everything is.'

Generosity is a wonderful way to build a consciousness of prosperity, since the very act of giving something away makes you feel as if you can afford more than you thought previously, and helps you overcome any insecure feelings of scarcity. By being generous, you demonstrate your faith in the free-flowing abundance of the universe. When you offer money, help, advice or support without any strings attached, you activate the law of giving and receiving, of cause and effect. You prosper by being generous and fail by being frugal. Giving is not losing. Giving is creating a positive karma. Whatever you give is a gift to yourself because the more you give the more you stimulate your own prosperity. The more you give the more you keep. As John Bunyan wrote:

> There was a man and they called him mad.
> The more he gave, the more he had.

When you think how best you can serve other people's higher good, you align yourself with the stream of life – you actually cooperate with God. In the words of the Bible, 'you can become rich by being generous or poor by being greedy' (Proverbs 11:24). You make a living with what you get, but you make a life with what you give.

In fact, tithing (giving a tenth of the income to charity) is an important religious precept in Judaism, Christianity and Islam. Give without thoughts of reward or recognition because every donation is secretly registered in the divine ledger for future remuneration. 'And when you do your

87

alms do not sound a trumpet before thee' (Matthew 6:2). Contribute without ulterior motives. Make giving its own reward by enjoying it. To prosper you must be generous. And do not worry. No matter how lavishly you give, you cannot outgive God. The more you give, the more you receive. Heed the words of Edwin Markham:

> There is a destiny that makes us brothers;
> No man goes his way alone;
> All that we send into the life of others
> Comes back into our own.

Your livelihood does not depend on your job. It is an illusion to think that you depend financially on other people such as your boss, your clients or your associates. Your income only seems to come from men, but it is not actually from men. We are all amply provided by a loving and generous Providence. And we each receive according to our acceptance of its endless exuberance. We each prosper according to the size of our consciousness – that is, according to how much we feel we deserve and how much we allow ourselves to receive. Successful people are no more deserving than others. They simply open themselves up to receive more, by feeling at one with the infinite source. They choose to believe that prosperity is theirs for the asking. Ultimately, it is our choices that make our lives.

Jealousy is a great pitfall to prosperity. Resenting someone else's success is a prescription for failure because it comes from the ego's fearful concept of scarcity. It makes you feel stressed, as if the supply of the universe is about to run out, leaving you deprived. And when your mind is focused on limits and scarcities, that is what you attract. Jealousy is a cry for more self-love, because it reflects a part of you that feels inadequate. Sometimes jealousy can get even deeper. It can say things like, 'I resent what you have even if I cannot have it,' or 'How dare you be more successful than me?' Such feelings are a manifestation of a spiritual dysfunction because they deny your divine identity of universal love and limitlessness. In fact, rejoicing in another's success actually works in your favour; when you are happy for someone else's prosperity, you are evolving your own prosperity consciousness. You thus allow it into your experience, knowing that the same power that prospered other people works equally for you too. Do not hold yourself back from affluence just because you suspect that it is not morally virtuous. Money is not the root of evil. Greed is. If used lovingly, money is love in action.

Have you noticed how many successful people hardly seem to work? These people have learned the secret of effortless creativity by flowing with life, rather than resisting it. Life naturally provides the fulfilment of our desires. Nature itself works in an effortless way. 'Consider the lilies in the field how they grow, they toil not, they spin not' (Luke 12:27). Realise that you do not make the crops grow. You only plant the seeds. Likewise, you can plant a seed of an idea in the fertile soil of your mind to grow any goal you desire. Sooner or later, your mind stuff becomes physical stuff.

Imagine that the president of a major car manufacturing company dreams up a new car with some sweeping technical novelties, far beyond conventional standards. So what does he do about it? First, he calls up his chief designer. He describes his dream car in detail and asks him to prepare an accurate drawing. The president then calls a general meeting of all the department managers, gives each a drawing of the new car and instructs them to outline a plan for its production. Obviously, many and varied technical and commercial factors have to be considered. Technical issues such as comfortable driving, safety features and manoeuvrability have to be coordinated with commercial aspects such as cost-effectiveness, promotion and marketing. All these complex issues must be resolved before the first new car can roll off the assembly line. But during all this time is the president worried about sorting out all these problems? Does he sweat the small stuff? Of course not. Once he has visualised the new car and set new targets for his work force, he stands back, trusting his engineers to solve all the problems involved in its creation.

We are all company presidents. We all have at our disposal a huge work force. We each have within us a creative power of infinite wisdom which is always ready to execute our dreams easily and effortlessly. Anything is possible, even that which may seem incredible or unrealistic to our intellect. All we need do is have a clear picture of a specific goal and trust that in its own time, it will be actualised. We thus outline a course of action for our divine work force. We thus set a direction for our infinite creativity. Clear pictures, however, are essential. Blurred or fuzzy pictures won't work. Focus, faith and patience release a tremendous creative power.

Everywhere we go we see hectic people rushing about as if trying to meet some imaginary deadlines. Hurry-sickness and over exertion are common fear symptoms. As Dr Ingrid Bacci writes in *The Art of Effortless Living*, 'The commitment to letting go of effort is the cornerstone of undoing the addiction to fear.' Tense efforts make any achievement harder. When you grip a pen you can hardly write. In our culture, hard work is a virtue and many people become obsessively occupied with their careers. Overly busy people are not using their time efficiently. They are not being creative. Time is the ally of imaginative people who dedicate part of each day to quit doing and practise *being*. To be more efficient it is better to put less effort into making the trek and more into reading the map. It is in the calm state of *being* that we can see the bigger picture. It is in the stillness of inactivity that we can hear the brilliant creative ideas of our inner guidance, saving us a lot of needless doing.

Nature creates effortlessly through the power of love. When our aspirations are motivated by love, not by greed or fear, we can similarly achieve our goals with the least effort. Our inner creativity knows how to accomplish things easily. When we realise this, we do not have to labour by the sweat of the brow. Not that there is any disgrace in physical work. City people give up office jobs and go 'back to nature' to become organic farmers and dig in the dirt. It is when we hate our work or resist it that it becomes a burden. Confucius said, 'Choose a job you love, and you will never have to work a day in your life.' Work can then be a joy, not an onerous strain. As Kahlil Gibran wrote in *The Prophet*, 'Work is love made visible.'

Imagination is one of the greatest gifts of human beings. Whatever we imagine, we can create by visualising it. Creative visualisation is a magical technique which uses mental images to create prosperity and, indeed, any goal. It uses the principle of *like attracts like*. A thought that has a certain vibration attracts a reality of a similar vibration, just like a radio receiver which, when tuned to a certain wavelength, will only receive the broadcast of a station of the same frequency, but not of any other. Likewise, to be able to attract, to make visualisation work for you, you must be very clear, very specific, very tuned. You must know exactly what your goal is and be able to make a mental picture of it.

If it is a new house you want, you have to visualise the house in all its glorious details. In your mind see the entrance, the furniture and the garden and bring yourself to feel as if you are living in it and enjoying its comforts. Trust that as you visualise it, it is yours. And do not worry where it is coming from, because this breaks the spell. It is best to

91

visualise when you are alone and calm in a quiet place where you can meditate on your goal without outer distractions. Just before bedtime or first thing in the morning when you are most relaxed are good times to do it. These are times when your mind is most receptive and your intellect is less likely to resist your optimistic aspirations.

Faith in your own creative power is crucial. When you believe, you release a powerful magnetising power in your mind. William James, the famous American psychologist, said, 'Our belief at the beginning of a doubtful undertaking is *the one thing* that ensures the successful outcome of the venture.' Cultivating belief in your goal is of utmost importance, because when you set yourself an ambitious aim, there is usually no way you can figure out how to create the means to get it. That is when your logic steps in, sowing doubts in your mind and weakening your resolve. When a destructive thought creeps in telling you that this is all nonsense, or what a fool you are, immediately push it out of mind with a positive thought. You must be alert not to let negative thoughts to take hold. You must have faith in the unlimited power of your unconscious mind, the seat of your creativity, to make things happen by devising intricate situations and coincidences way beyond your ability to comprehend. All you need do is hold the vision every day and allow yourself to be led. Do not intervene in the process. If you do, you block the creative flow.

Just as sceptical attitudes of mind obstruct the creative channel, dynamic actions of faith expand it. The following old Hassidic story illustrates how a demonstration of faith can make a burning desire come true.

Two pious brothers who travelled every year on the harvest festival to visit their teacher used to stay overnight at the same inn, eventually becoming friends with the innkeeper. One year, as they arrived at the inn, they found their innkeeper friend looking downcast and listless. After much persuasion the innkeeper revealed that he was depressed about his wife's infertility. He said, 'My wife wants so much to become a mother. She has been trying for years to become pregnant but up to now we have not been successful. I heard that your master works miracles and that his prayers are powerful. Do you think he might be willing to pray for us?' So the brothers promised him to ask their teacher to include them in his prayers.

The next morning, as the brothers were getting ready to depart, they were amazed to see the innkeeper's wife walking about the village with a brand new baby's pram! When people congratulated her on her new baby she would say: 'Oh, no, I do not have a baby yet.' The villagers would then pitifully nod their heads, thinking that her craving for a baby had probably made her lose her mind. The brothers were also concerned because at that time, prams were an expensive luxury and the innkeeper's wife must have spent most of her savings to buy it. However, since nothing could be done, the brothers went on their way.

At the next harvest festival, when the brothers set to travel again to their master, they hesitated to go to the same inn, fearing not to be so welcome if the innkeeper's wife had not conceived. They decided therefore to proceed cautiously and to call only if they heard a baby crying. However, as they reached the inn, they found themselves in the midst of a jubilant birth celebration. Being warmly welcome, they were made godfathers of the newborn child. Although the brothers were happy for the new parents, one of them could not help feel a twinge of sadness. As soon as they arrived at their teacher's house, this brother requested an urgent audience with his master. He entered the room of his revered teacher with tears in his eyes, asking: 'Am I not important to you? Am I a lesser man than the innkeeper? My wife and I wanted a child as well. I have asked you to pray for my wife every year for the past decade. You have agreed but we are still childless. But when you prayed for this innkeeper who is not your loyal disciple and whom you do not even know, his wife had a baby within a year.' Looking at his old pupil with great compassion in his eyes, the master asked: 'Tell me, my dear friend and disciple, did your wife ever go out to buy a baby's pram?'

To reach a goal we have to demonstrate our faith in it. We must overcome any niggling misgivings by taking positive action. Any act of faith we do helps to impress our mind and reinforce our commitment. Just like the woman in the story, we need to buy the metaphorical pram where there is no sign of pregnancy. Faith attracts, doubt repels. According to Shakespeare, our doubts are our traitors. So make sure you do not betray your cherished aspirations. When you doubt whether you can attain your goal, you are failing yourself.

To achieve, give up control. Learn to flow patiently with whatever transpires. The Buddhists have an expression: 'Don't push the river. It will travel in its own speed anyway.' Once you set a goal, let go of any emotional attachments to it. Do not stress yourself wondering what if it does not happen. Be firm, but flexible. Think *que sera, sera.* When you are not compulsively attached to your goal and do not try to figure out ways to get it, you step into the field of all possibilities. You allow magic.

You must keep your faith even if the flow of events seems to take you temporarily in a totally different direction, and it looks as if the goal is getting away from you. Sometimes, the complex way is the only way to the simple place. Trust that in the long run, the process will be more effective and effortless than it would have been by struggling and striving. Get excited about the experience. Think of it as an adventure. Use affirmations to bolster your faith in your creative power. Be aware that by merely having an intention, you are giving a direction to this hidden power. To put it in the

94

words of the great painter Paul Cézanne, 'What we vividly imagine, ardently desire and enthusiastically act upon, must inevitably come to pass.'

Sometimes you may choose a goal which is not right for you or your higher purpose. This happens when your goal is not soul-oriented but ego-oriented. Once you have a clear desire, allow yourself to be led. Allow the universe to lead you to your desire in its own way and be willing to accept whatever transpires. You may, for example, ask for a great deal of money, but your higher self may decide that you are not ready to handle it, or that it will not serve your higher good. It may also be that your attitude needs changing or that you have conflicting concepts that are blocking the creative energy. The universe will delay the process and send you other lessons to prepare you for your initial goal. Think of the universe as a loving teacher who will give you the things you want only when you are ready; only when you will not be harmed by what you want. Trust that your request is heard, and if you do not receive exactly what you asked for, you will receive the essence of your wish or the stages that will prepare you for it. Remember that God is good and wise in what He gives and what He denies.

Integrity in business dealings is very important when you aspire for prosperity. By paying your debts in time and keeping your promises you are activating the law of cause and effect in your behalf. You are sending a message to your unconscious mind that you mean what you say. By honouring your commitments to other people you create a positive karma. You are embracing the Taoist principle of *attracting the positive with positive.* By treating others with honesty, you create a cause which will attract its appropriate effect. Other people will in turn be true to you and reciprocate your actions.

Integrity is also a way to become whole. It is a way to realise your full potential. To integrate means to unite or complete. By practising integrity in daily life you unite all the parts of your personality. You become complete and therefore more powerful, because you can face life with all your potential. Dishonest dealings break down your wholeness into parts and weaken your power.

Appreciation and gratitude can open many prosperity channels for you and send out a call to the universe to give you more. So make it a habit to thank God for every gift that you receive and it will attract more of the same. With gratitude and appreciation you can bypass your ego, heal your emotions, raise your energy and attract higher and better things into your life.

7

Love and Heal Yourself

Love is a powerful healing energy. Healers can heal because they can harness and channel healing energy, a life-force of a very high frequency, higher than that of the person being treated. In recent years, various studies of mind–body connection are increasingly confirming the ancient concept that spiritual healing is not something mystical, but is a practical alternative therapy. The word *healing* comes from the Anglo-Saxon word *healan*, which combines both body and spirit. Aspiring to promote health and well-being is one of the best practices of self-love.

In this sense, there is a difference between healing procedures and spontaneous curing. Although occasionally, miraculous cures from debilitating diseases do happen following a deep spiritual experience, as sometimes take place in holy sites such as Lourdes, healing involves the practice of rectifying the cause of physical disorders in order to reach a state of well-being.

The greatest medicine is something you cannot see or touch. It is your mind power. It is the energy of your spirit. It is in your awareness of the life-force, called *chi* by the Chinese or *prana* by the Indians, that flows through your body and which can help heal any disorder if only you believe in it and cooperate with it.

In fact, faith healing was the dominant form of treatment in ancient Greece as far back as 500 BC. Pythagoras, the sixth-century BC. mathematician, philosopher and physician, considered mind and body to be integrated, and healing to be a most sublime form of treatment. He said, 'There is no illness, only ignorance,' referring to ignorance as our separation from our spirit by ignoring our connection to our spiritual higher self. It was only later that Hippocrates penned his *Hippocratic Corpus*, separating physical health from spirituality, thus laying the foundation for modern medicine.

The revival of interest in spiritual healing is due, at least in part, to the New Age movement, although New Age healing has more in common with Jungian psychology. New Age holds that most diseases are psychologically rooted and that traumatic experiences need to be healed first, before physical health can be restored. It deals, therefore, with healing the so-called emotional hurts. Other healers maintain that physical health constantly mirrors spiritual attitudes of mind. They claim that disease is the result of some spiritual or mental aberration and that inner dis-harmony is reflected in physical dis-ease. Every disease is a wake-up call; every disorder has a message. To heal, a patient should do some soul-searching. He or she should analyse their lives and try to look for the higher cause of their condition. Mentally resisting people and events is resisting life itself. Stress, fear, worry, anxiety, repressed anger and long-held grudges are obstacles to the flow of life-energy and can trigger a vast array of diseases, from asthma to cancer. Such lower emotions are unloving ways to treat the body. *A Course in Miracles* states: 'Health is the result of relinquishing all attempts to use the body lovelessly.' Self-love and self acceptance are crucial for your mental and physical health because they allow your energy to flow freely.

Illness is a complex issue. People get sick for various reasons. Emotional imbalance, physical problems, genetic defects or hereditary faults are just a few of the main causes.

Conventional medicine, however, conceives of the body as a complex apparatus comprising different departments as separate, independent parts. As a result, doctors specialise in treating different organs. A cardiologist will only treat your heart and a gastroenterologist will only deal with your digestive system. In contrast, holistic medicine sees body, mind and soul as one wholeness, an interconnected system in which anything that happens in one part has an impact on other parts. Mind affects body and body affects mind. As the ancient Chinese medicine proverb states, 'Where the mind goes, the body follows.' The human body is perceived as an energy field, constantly flowing life energy, in which any energy blockage along its flow, such as in Chinese acupuncture meridians or Indian Chakras, causes disease. New healing modalities of energy psychology such as EFT (Emotional Freedom Technique) and TAT (Tapas Acupressure Technique), which involve simple finger tapping of acupressure points with affirmations of self-love, are actually demonstrating that by clearing emotional debris and streamlining the flow of the body's energy along its meridian pathways, many and varied chronic conditions, from depression and phobias to migraines and allergies, can be healed within minutes. Past-life therapy is now becoming increasingly popular when a disease defies all medical treatments and its causes cannot be identified. Having said that, it is important to remember that adopting alternative procedures should not mean rejecting conventional medicine. Healing therapies are best combined with medical treatments.

Forgiveness has great healing powers. When disease occurs, one of the common lessons it teaches is to learn to forgive others as well as ourselves. It is time to release repressed resentments and grudges which dim the aura and poison the body. When you do not forgive someone who has harmed you in the past, you are punishing yourself in the present. Think of this absurdity: You are hurting yourself for the wrongdoings of another person! Forgiveness heals, blame ails. Although it may not be easy, try to bless this person and release them from your life with love. If someone ripped you off, know that in the long run, nobody can take away from you anything which is yours by right of consciousness. If it is truly yours, it will return to you. In the meantime, learn to free yourself from the heavy emotional burden of animosity, resentment, revenge or self-pity. By choosing to send love to whoever wronged you, you are actually giving yourself a gift. You are raising the vibration of your spirit and healing your life.

In view of the fantastic achievements of modern medicine in eradicating the plagues of the past, overcoming infections and extending life-span, we might wonder how it is that according to recent statistics one in every three patients turns to alternative medicine. Why are complementary therapies becoming so popular?

Well, in spite of the developments of wonder drugs, magical surgeries and fabulous diagnostic techniques, average health *quality* has been declining. True, we no longer suffer from smallpox or bubonic plague. But we have instead plagues of heart attacks, cancer and strokes. And all because medicine, although being very efficient in curing diseases that are caused by germs, is very inefficient in curing diseases that are caused by much more complex causes, such as high blood pressure, migraines or arthritis. Today you are considered a healthy person by your doctor even if you suffer from nervousness, depression, allergies, constipation, premenstrual tension, poor libido, six colds a year, constant tiredness and a feeling of impending doom. But people are no longer agreeing to put up with these miseries, and they do not want to hear their doctor telling them, 'It's all in your mind,' or 'Take a vacation.' More and more people are not willing to accept the medical definition of health, which is absence of a full-blown disease or a collection of minor symptoms. They simply want a positive feeling of well-being. Is it any wonder so many people are crowding into health food stores and flocking to alternative practitioners?

Consulting with a professional nutritionist or reading nutrition books, improving eating habits and eliminating stressing foods like sugar, coffee and alcohol from the diet can help alleviate stress and calm anger and restlessness. Foods that release serotonin (a calming brain chemical), like bananas, milk and potatoes, supplements of B complex vitamins, vitamin C, calcium and zinc, can help strengthen the nervous system and make it easier for the body to cope with distressing emotions such as tension and anxiety. (For more information, see my book *Complete Nutrition*.)

Choosing healthy foods is an act of self-love. Just as you can choose love over hate, so you can choose nourishing foods over junk foods. Although food is primarily meant to be a life-sustaining nourishment, we use food for a variety of emotional reasons. We often substitute food for love and become overweight. We use comfort eating to overcome distress and fear. Some people binge on chocolate following a broken love affair. Others use alcohol as a form of escapism to drown their sorrows, release inhibitions or just to cheer themselves up. Gourmets often indulge in eating for mere pleasure. Although food should be tasty and eating should be enjoyable, there is no need to wallow in overly fatty, salty or sugary foods just to gratify taste buds. Many health food dishes are simply delicious as well as nutritious. Self-loving people eat to live, while careless people live to eat. Overindulging in refined, empty-calorie foods just for fun usually leads to wrong food choices which result in nutritional deficiency symptoms, low energy, poor health and becoming overweight.

Obesity is a new world plague. The World Health Organisation (WHO) warned in 2005 that more than a billion adults are considered overweight and at least 300 million of them are obese. Child obesity is spiralling. In December 2002, a UK parliamentary report warned that ten per cent of the children in Britain are obese and forty per cent do not eat fruit and vegetables every day. Obesity is a major contributing cause of a cluster of critical diseases. People suffering from conditions like diabetes, hypertension, heart disease, strokes, arthritis and cancer, all related to their excess weight, are increasingly turning to courts to sue major food companies that sell processed foods high in sugar and saturated fats. Long-ignored warnings from nutritionists are now falling on attentive ears. It has been recently reported that some of the world's major food manufacturers, including Kellogg, Nestlé and Kraft, pledged to reduce or eliminate the use of hydrogenated oils, the so-called *killer fats*, which are associated with obesity, high cholesterol levels, clogged arteries, heart attacks, strokes and death. McDonald's is substituting lard with vegetable oil. Kraft foods is also planning to reduce sugar and salt, as well as the portion size of some snacks. The fast food industry seems now likely to be forced to make its products healthier. But you do not have to wait for them to make better food choices. Anyone can choose to eat healthily right now, adopting a natural and wholesome diet high in fresh fruit and vegetables.

To keep healthy, the immune system must function at peak performance. An efficient immune system will engulf and destroy hostile bugs and viruses, and kill cancer cells as they are formed. It will also help generate more energy and sustain a feeling of well-being. Many people are concerned about being exposed to germs and try to shun them. But germs are everywhere, so how come people are not sick all the time? The answer is that most healthy people have a good immune response which protects the body from hostile invaders. Remember that even during flu epidemics not everyone gets sick. There are those people with strong immunity who remain healthy throughout the flu season. The same was true even during the days of the Black Plague which, although it wiped out millions of people, still did not kill everyone. Parts of the population seemed to show greater resistance than others. The best health insurance is therefore in developing a strong immunity.

Although a strong immune system depends to a great extent on the genes you inherited, there is still a lot anyone can do to bolster natural defences. Positive emotions, cheerful attitudes of mind, sensible lifestyle, adequate sleep and exercise, good food choices and nutritional supplementation all lead to higher immunity. The immune system, however, is highly complex and is affected by myriad factors, from food to mood. An attitude of self-love, though, is a basic requirement. When you love yourself enough, you will put your well-being at the top of your priority ladder. You will not abuse your body with drinking and smoking. You will skip junk foods and adopt healthy eating habits which boost your immune response.

In spiritual terms, diseases are created in various parts of the body by a contraction of energy which occurs when the life energy in a certain area of the body drops to a low level. Disease is a great teacher of self-love. A common cold, for example, can remind you to slow down, rest, let go of some of the pressure you are under and nurture yourself more, things that you may have neglected to do. Some diseases are created for the same reason you create any other crisis – to provide you with an opportunity to release old negative concepts and rise to a new level of self-love and self-acceptance. When you love yourself more, when you honour your needs more, you raise the frequency of your energy, allowing the contracted area the chance to expand and heal. In this sense, a healing session can be very helpful, as a healer has a much greater capacity to channel high vibration energy to a patient which, in turn, helps clear up blocked areas and creates an opportunity for healing.

Emotions trigger biochemical reactions. Thoughts can release either stress hormones like cortisol or feel-good hormones like endorphins. Unloving emotions such as distress, insecurity or fear weaken the immune system and increase vulnerability to disease, whereas loving emotions like joy and optimism boost immune activity. For better or for worse, every cell and organ is affected by emotions. Emotionally induced diseases, referred to by the medical profession as psychosomatic disorders, are well documented in medical literature. The first step in healing is to heal the emotions. And in that sense, the mind is the greatest healer (see Chapter 16, 'The Healing Mind' in my book *Complete Nutrition*).

Fear, the opposite of love, has been recognised throughout history as the underlying cause of many afflictions. In primitive tribes, witch doctors used weird rituals to rid sick people of 'evil spirits', or fears. Resentments and grudges are also well-known ailing emotions. By resisting life's events, they create energy stoppages in different parts of the body which give rise to many and varied conditions. Repressed resentment and prolonged grief are now recognised as some of the major contributing causes of cancer. By resenting a situation, someone's behaviour or even something you yourself did, you create inner pain. This pain is reminding you to stop resisting the flow of life and practise a faithful acceptance of whatever is happening. In a difficult situation remember the famous prayer:

> God, grant me the serenity to accept
> The things I cannot change,
> The courage to change the things I can
> And the wisdom to know the difference.

Anger is one of the symptoms of fear. An outburst of anger can shoot blood pressure up to dangerous levels. Susceptible people can end up with a heart attack. When anger is turned inward – that is, when you do not allow yourself to express anger – anger turns into depression. It is therefore important to release anger. Letting your feelings out is great for purging yourself of festering emotions. Find a method that suits you best. Yell, beat up pillows, do push ups or go to the gym for a workout. Learn to say to an offending person, 'I am angry with you.' In her seminars, Dr Elizabeth Kübler-Ross has a special method to release anger which she calls *externalisation*. She has people each take a piece of rubber hose and start beating up old phone books over and over. Once pent-up anger is released, the situation can be seen from a different point of view and new insights can come to light.

Prolonged or excessive stress is a common scourge of civilisation. At one time or another we are all affected by it, especially when we have to endure adverse events which seem out of our control. Sometimes, a little bit of pressurised excitement, however, can spice up life and can also serve as a positive motivator. Stress becomes harmful, though, only when continuous daily strains overwhelm the body's balancing systems. It is important to recognise the first warning signs of stress and how it affects health. It might be tiredness, sleeplessness, headaches, an outbreak of eczema or diarrhoea. It might be emotional changes such as moodiness and irritability which are sometimes more noticeable to others than to us. Long-term stress can be manifested in various diseases like hypertension, duodenal ulcers, irritable bowel syndrome, psoriasis and menstrual disorders. Stress management involves changing your thinking patterns and improving your lifestyle. Relaxation techniques, breathing exercises, yoga, meditation, reading self-help books or practising tai-chi are some of the best ways to relieve stress.

Worry is a common distressing emotion which can ruin the quality of life. It is a fear-based emotion, the fear of the unknown. When you are worried or fearful, you forget how much you are looked after by your spirit; you are unaware of life's great caring love that always follows you like a shadow, never leaving you. Remember that however dark your path seems, the light is still there. Just like a sun which is obscured by an overcast sky, your own light is only shaded by the clouds of your experience. As the clouds move away, the light will shine again in your life. So stop worrying and start living.

To dispel the darkness of distressing emotions we need to shed light on them. We can begin by acknowledging their existence. Just naming them can help a lot. As Carl Jung said, 'One does not become enlightened by imagining figures of light but by making the darkness conscious.' When you acknowledge the problem, you are on the way to solving it. Many people who undergo a crisis, however, try to hide their vulnerability as if it was something shameful. They would put up a brave face, saying, for example, 'I am not afraid' when they are, or 'I do not worry' when they do. By living in denial they are blocking the solution. Without an emotional outlet they are simply locking their predicament deeper within. Do not be afraid to look vulnerable. You will feel relieved once you air your plight. And you will thus clear up your emotional system as well as warm up your relationships with others.

Many people are not aware of the many advantages that life has bestowed on them, particularly in times of adversity, when they are stressed and worried and can hardly think about anything else. They do not appreciate basic but precious things like their eyesight, their intelligence, their family or their freedom. They take everything for granted. They forget that even in the midst of their crisis, there are people much worse off than them out there who would gladly swap places with them anytime. To de-stress, start counting your blessings. The more often you do this, the better you will feel. It will put your present difficulty in the right perspective and make you realise that in spite of everything, you still have a lot to be grateful for.

Alternative medicine is now becoming more established, as an increasing number of therapies are now supported by scientific evidence. One article, for example, in the August 2000 edition of the *British Medical Journal*, showed that homoeopathy can alleviate allergic rhinitis (inflammation of nose membranes). Likewise, acupuncture was found to help relieve morning sickness of pregnancy. The present trend is to combine holistic therapies with medical treatments in what is called *integrated medicine*. In the United Kingdom, 37 per cent of NHS doctors are now using homoeopathy in their practices. Indeed, more and more medical doctors are referring patients to various alternative therapies, ranging from reflexology and acupuncture to rolfing and Indian head massage. Not surprisingly, this alternative approach is now being adopted by insurance companies that sell income protection policies, which pay out a salary if you are sick and off work for a prolonged period of time. It is in the interest of these insurers to get people back to work as soon as possible and stop claiming insurance pay-outs, so they are willing to cover any alternative therapy that can help overcome your stress, bad back or whatever condition is keeping you from work.

Exercise complements sound eating habits and a sensible lifestyle. Regular exercise is generally known to increase fitness, relieve fatigue, control weight and stimulate bowel movement. But this is only the tip of the iceberg. On the physical side, studies have shown that regular exercise lowers high cholesterol levels, reduces hypertension, tones the heart and alleviates respiratory disorders. Aerobic exercise is known to save people from heart attacks. Gym workout can help prevent or combat osteoporosis, especially common in post-menopausal women. On the psychological side, exercise was found to relieve stress or depression because it stimulates the release of endorphins, the feel-good hormones which account for the elated feeling after a workout. (For more information, see Chapter 20 of *Complete Nutrition*.)

Sad, fearful or depressive thoughts can make you ill. A research conducted by the American neuroscientist Dr Richard Davison with two groups of people showed that intense negative thinkers have poorer immune reactions, whereas optimistic people who habitually recall happy events in their lives have higher levels of antibodies and increased immune response against disease.

In fact, pessimism is a killer. A newly published long-term study conducted at the Mayo Clinic in Minnesota, which tracked the lives of 800 people during 30 years, revealed that pessimists are almost 20 per cent more likely to die young than optimists. One of the researchers, Dr Toshihiko Maruta, said, 'Wellness is not just physical, but attitudinal. How you perceive what goes on around you and how you interpret it may have an impact on your longevity, and can also affect the quality of your later years. It is possible to improve health just by being more optimistic.' Professor Cary Cooper, an expert on health psychology at Lancaster University, said: 'An optimist will think, "I can change this, I can do something about it." But a pessimist will think that they can't control anything.' Recommended tip: Surround yourself with upbeat people and make a note of three positive things that happen to you each day.

Laughter is the best medicine. Laughter, especially in the form of belly laughs, was scientifically found to create a feeling of pleasure and optimism by stimulating the secretion of brain endorphins. Laughter is not only the best antidote to depression and pessimism, it is also a powerful therapeutic tool. Back in the 1970s, Dr Norman Cousins, author of *Anatomy of an Illness*, showed how he managed to heal himself from ankylosing spondylitis – a debilitating disease of the vertebrae for which the doctors had no cure – with laughter and vitamin C. To keep himself laughing, he used to order comedy movies to watch in the hospital and ask visitors to come up with jokes. And in November 2006, the *Daily Mail* reported that a mother in a two-year coma lying in hospital with brain damage caused by a car accident, was going home after her son made her laugh. Comedy can deflect misery.

Indeed, a little humour in daily life can go a long way to help release tension. It helps cope with whatever life throws at us. Being able to laugh about unfortunate or irritating events is a great asset. It helps you to see things in proportion. It helps keep you sane when everything around you gets crazy.

The more you practise looking for the funny side or the ludicrous in every situation, the better you become at spotting it. Adding a slant of humour to anything that crops up makes you realise, as the saying goes, that life is too important to be taken seriously.

Common daily trifles can be stressing if you allow them to be. Our quick pace of life has resulted in many stressing occupations, especially when deadlines have to be met constantly. Even simple things like driving a car in the rush hour can be straining. Many occupations can be stressing. With the build up in the body of stress hormones like adrenalin and cortisol, which are not diffused by physical exertion, the pent-up stress can become a serious health hazard. It can cause many related conditions, from heart-burn to heart disease and from a migraine to a stroke, unless offset by some humour.

So take life more light-heartedly. Try to find a funny bit in whatever you do. Be creative. You do not have to memorise jokes like a professional comedian, but you can make up your private cracks in your own daily life. I once heard about a very busy psychiatric clinic which installed a new automatic phone switchboard with pre-recorded out-going messages as follows:

Hello. Thank you for calling. Please listen carefully to our list of options and press the appropriate button:

- If you are obsessive, press 1 repeatedly.
- If you are co-dependent, get someone else to press 2.
- If you have multiple personalities, press 3, 5 and 8.
- If you are paranoid, we know who you are and why you are calling. Just stay on the line and we will trace your call.
- If you are depressed, it does not matter which number you press, because we will not answer anyway.

This is an example how to use a bit of jollity in pro-fessional life and reduce tension in a highly stressful occupation.

Life itself offers many amusing situations, if only we are alert enough to notice them. A devout Catholic mother, for example, overheard her child praying at bedtime: 'Dear God, please look after my dad who works two jobs and after my mum who looks after me and my sister, please also look after my granny who can barely see and after aunt Jennie who limps with a cane. And God, please look after yourself, because if something happens to you, we are all sunk.'

Pain, discomfort and illness are the body's frantic calls to alert us to problems which must be rectified. They are the body's last resort to get our attention, if we would only listen. Our immunity system aspires to keep us healthy, constantly working hard to mend the damage caused by any offensive habits we practise. If, however, you abuse your body excessively, beyond its ability to repair, such as by extended smoking, drinking or stress, you eventually create a full-blown disease.

At the first sign of pain or discomfort, however, many will rush to the medicine cabinet for a painkiller. The pill will abate the pain for a while but will not solve the underlying problem. This is like saying to the body, 'Shut up, I do not want to listen to you.' Many would rather play victim than make the effort to heed the message. The body may be telling you to cut down drinking, quit smoking, avoid junk food or just slow down, relax and have a good night's sleep. Alternatively, it may be warning you to get a medical check-up. The body does want to get well. But it is up to you to cooperate with it.

It is important to realise that just as we create life crises to teach us much-needed lessons, so too we create illnesses to discard unloving attitudes, to let go of fears, reduce tension and rise to a higher level of self-love. Putting our priorities right is of utmost importance. The mere intent to make health your top priority has an immense impact. The body cells will heed this call and will act in compliance. You will be amazed at how new ideas will start flowing into your mind. Ideas that will lead you to improve your health, boost your energy and increase your feeling of well-being. You can have anything you want just by wanting it. You have the right of choice. You can choose positive desires to get positive results. So decide to get rid of self-defeating thoughts. Choose your wants carefully. Emerson said, 'Beware of what you want, for you will get it.'

Sleep is a great healer. According to the president of the Royal Society of Medicine, we now sleep two hours less each night than our grandparents did. It seems that we prefer to have fun, surf the net, overwork or do something 'constructive' with our time. Staying up late is a sign of sophistication, as only simpletons are supposed to go to bed early. So we delude ourselves that sleep is a waste of time. We are wrong. Many of us unknowingly suffer from sleep deprivation, which explains why so many people are often unfocused, dizzy or weary. No wonder that it is now estimated that more people are killed on our roads by tired drivers than by drunk ones.

To understand the importance of sleep we have only to see what happens to sleep-deprived people. During the Korean war, atrocious experiments in sleep deprivation with American POWs showed that they became easily prone to brainwashing and eventually died of exhaustion if prevented from sleeping for fourteen days. Subsequent research revealed that lesser degrees of sleep deprivation not only led to irritability, loss of concentration and metabolic disturbances, they also weakened the immune system. After a few nights of inadequate or disturbed sleep, many people became prone to catch cold. Sleep deprivation is now suspected to be linked to diabetes and obesity. Disrupted sleep patterns in people who work shifts is known to increase the risk of cardiovascular disease. Adequate sleep is therefore imperative for a healthy feeling of well-being and efficient work, whereas inadequate sleep can turn us into a sick society.

Visualising yourself as a healthily active person can promote healing of diseases by stimulating the body's great mechanisms of self-repair. Physiology itself is an amazing intelligence in action, under which body cells constantly communicate with each other to perform life-sustaining processes. A fantastic healing power is inbred in every cell. All that is required is to muster the energy that boosts this healing power. Visualisation is so powerful to effect cures and healing because our unconscious mind, the inner wis-

112

dom which regulates all physiological functions like computer software, has a certain 'flaw': It cannot distinguish between a vivid mental vision and an actual physical experience. It interprets them both as default programming for future operation. Visualising yourself enjoying a healthy lifestyle can make you feel elated whether you actually felt it physically or just imagined it. To take advantage of this attribute, just sit or lie down totally relaxed, preferably at bedtime or first thing in the morning, and visualise yourself healthy and energetic, pursuing all your favourite activities. This can be enhanced by repeating an affirmation about the positive state of your health.

In recent years various reports were published about terminal cancer patients who succeeded in combating cancer by positive visualisation. Books like *Getting Well Again* by Dr Carl Simonton or *Living Loving and Healing* by Dr Bernie Siegel offer various visualisation techniques for people with cancer which often produce great results. Also available are audiotapes with guidance on visualisation and meditation.

Obviously, visualisations are only supposed to enhance a conventional medical treatment, not to replace it. It is important to choose a visualisation that you feel comfortable with. Some people, for example, visualise the immune system's natural killer (NK) cells engulfing and destroying cancer cells, thus intensifying the job that the NKs are naturally supposed to do. Then there are those who prefer to imagine sun rays melting cancerous tumours, while others visualise a waterfall washing away the cancer cells.

Health affirmations can help a lot, too. When done consistently they gradually permeate the unconscious mind like mental osmosis. The body cells accept these affirmations as commands and tend to align themselves with their instruction. This gives a new specific direction to the healing energy. A classical affirmation for general use that stood

113

the test of time is by Emile Coué, the French pioneer of auto-suggestion psychotherapy:

> Every day and in every way,
> I am getting better,
> Better and better.

This affirmation is based on the concept that every person and, indeed, every living organism has the potential of divine wisdom. Its repetition has the power of a hypnotic suggestion. By reciting it several times a day, every day, you identify with your higher self and unleash its power to enhance health and spiritual confidence.

8

Living with Your Loved One

A loving and harmonious connection with a loved one is one of the greatest challenges of life. The gradual increase in divorce rates over the last few decades has reached such a high proportion that nowadays, divorce and separation are almost as widespread as marriage. People anticipate divorce even before marriage and prenuptial agreements are now increasingly considered as an acceptable and common procedure.

In past centuries, marriage was regarded as a sacred institution. People married for life and were expected by society to keep their vows and live together 'until death do us part'. Divorces were not only rare but also a stigma. When they occurred, they were a source of shame and embarrassment for the whole family. Why is it, then, that divorces are now so rampant and marriages evermore transient? Why is it that so many people attract incompatible partners? Why do people create painful relationships? Why is it that nowadays, when the first marital difficulty pops up, people are quicker to cop out of the relationship to separate and divorce, rather than face the challenge head on and sort out the problem?

Well, no relationship happens by chance or coincidence. We attract people who mirror something within us. We attract those people who are meant to teach us specific lessons that we need for our spiritual evolution. Many of us are sometimes led into painful relationships to help us recognise and heal unloving attitudes that are impeding our growth, with the purpose of leading us to a higher level of unconditional love and acceptance. In that sense, every relationship is actually a growth workshop in which difficulties are the assignments.

In the male-dominated societies of past centuries, most women endured the pains of an incompatible or abusive husband for a lifetime because without a husband, a woman literally had no social status. Only few women knew how to love and assert themselves and even fewer dared to challenge the system. Women have since claimed their self-value and have become emancipated. Simultaneously, the pace of life has become faster. Both men and women are now quick to learn from their relationships. They are more assertive and less inclined to put up with an incompatible partner or a painful relationship when it does not feel right anymore, which is why separations and divorces are now on the increase.

We attract friends and loved ones into our lives whose levels of spiritual growth and life lessons are similar to ours. Each one of us has a unique aura. Each one of us emits a specific energy signal.

We may be more developed than our loved ones in certain areas, while they may be more advanced than us in other ways. But we have transmitted a similar vibration or the connection would not have occurred. Our souls have led us to each other to teach us both what we need to learn in order to evolve our personality as well as our spirit. When that happens, we feel a 'chemistry' with the other person.

Learning to connect with other people in more loving ways helps us grow. When we want to increase harmony in our relationships, we must learn to allow other people to be who they are, and as we do, we also increase our own capacity to accept ourselves as we are, with all our imperfections included. Self-love and universal love are interconnected. Improving your relationships with others helps you improve your relationship with yourself.

To help yourself grow, frequently set aside time to spend quietly on your own. Calm your mind chatter, reflect about the inner meanings and morals of what's happening in your life, meditate, take a long walk in the woods or read inspirational books. Listen to your inner voice. As you do, you start developing an inner connection with your higher self, with the universe, with God. When you connect with God, you connect with the essence of love, because God is love. And a union with God promotes self-love because our soul is an individualised part of the divine. A higher state of self-love allows you to love more, to trust more, to keep your heart open and to create deeper and more meaningful relationships by reaching new levels of sharing and intimacy.

We are all fellow travellers on a learning path. Relationships and marriages challenge us to love one another unconditionally and learn to accept a spouse who thinks differently, reacts differently and behaves differently. They offer us the opportunity to expand our tolerance and increase our compassion. All relationships, however, are dynamic experiences. During any long-term relationship, people may change. They can alter their self-image, their views or even their personality. They may re-prioritise their values. All of a sudden, you get a strange feeling that you are with a person totally different from the one you first knew. Both of you start to see things differently. That is because one of you has not evolved at the same pace or in terms of the same issues as the other. As one partner grows faster than the other, he or she may rise to a higher vibration. When this occurs, couples usually separate. They have lost their attraction because their energies are no longer on the same wavelength.

A separation time, as painful as it may be, is again another opportunity to practise unconditional love. If you have outgrown your partner and feel that the relationship is no longer working and that you must split, do not be tempted to feel self-righteous or patronising, no matter how the other person acts. It is all too easy to fall into the trap of the blaming game. When you act in a condescending or resentful way you are decreasing your energy. You are closing your heart and lowering your vibration.

As a single person, you can enjoy the many comforts of your freedom. You can do as you please. There is no one else to consider. There is no need to compromise or make concessions in order to accommodate someone else. No need to make any sacrifices. You are your own master. So why would seemingly sane people give up all the privileges of freedom and commit themselves to the constraints of a relationship? Why are single people so eager to meet someone that they flock to subscribe to dating agencies, surf the Internet or scan social columns in newspapers? You know the answer: they are all looking for the love that will stir the cockles of their hearts. They want to experience moments of bliss. They are in pursuit of happiness, sharing and intimacy. They want to expand emotionally. But actually, any relationship is a spiritual growth academy which teaches love and acceptance. In *The Road Less Traveled*, Dr M. Scott Peck says that love is more than an emotion, it is a decision to take on a responsibility. He defines love as: 'The will to extend one's self for the purpose of nurturing one's own or another's spiritual growth.' The problem is that many people see marriage with a loved one as a way to companionship and gratification. They are unaware of the call of their soul to extend, to heal and to grow. Such people miss the quintessence of their relationship.

To make a relationship work and enjoy its blessings, we have got to extend ourselves. We need to practise self-

118

discipline and be prepared to make efforts for the higher good of our partner. This is the tuition fee we pay for attending this course in spiritual growth. And as in any school, no one can guarantee that you will graduate with honours or even reach graduation at all. But to have a reasonable chance of success, two basic conditions are required: sincerity and determination. Sincerity in the intention to make the relationship work and determination to make the effort.

Taking your partner for granted is one of the greatest pitfalls in any relationship. A few years after falling in love and getting married, when the daily life of having a family and pursuing a career turns into a set routine, many people wake up one morning to find that there is no longer any romance in their lives. The flamboyant passion has gone. The joy and intimacy of their love has faded away. And familiarity may even breed contempt. This is when couples start growing apart, all because they forgot to extend themselves to keep their love alive. People who fall in love and live happily ever after exist only in fairy tales. Love involves a constant effort. It has been said that marriage is like reading a novel. If you put the book down long enough, you may lose the plot. Love implies constantly extending your limits by exceeding them. Love is a commitment to appreciate your loved one even as time and familiarity take their toll.

To keep romance in our life we need to be continuously romantic. We keep our love alive when we remember birthdays and anniversaries, when we buy flowers, when we say 'I love you,' when we surprise our loved one with an unexpected courtesy such as Sunday breakfast in bed or a romantic candlelit dinner. Most important of all is spending quality time together, setting aside time for intimate chats and sharing life's experiences. The flame of a relationship is fed by the oil of love.

119

To heal an ailing relationship start by healing yourself. Begin by opening up your heart. By shifting ego-oriented thoughts to higher and nobler views, you can begin to see your partner from a different aspect. From the ego's point of view, which is when your heart is closed, you find faults, you judge and you criticise: 'How dare he treat me like that', or 'She would rather gossip with her friends than prepare my dinner.' From the empathy of your higher self you open your heart to view your partner with unconditional love, compassion and understanding. If you remember that your partner's behaviour is actually mirroring something in your own attitudes, it is easier to be less judgemental. If you feel that you are not loved enough or are betrayed by your partner, go inwardly and check whether you love yourself enough and whether, in a certain way, you are not betraying your own values. Whatever the problem, find time to discuss it with your partner. Speak from your heart, listen with compassion. Share intimate hurts. A loving attitude can help heal emotional wounds and provide an opportunity for growth, whatever the disagreement. One of the greatest challenges of an ailing relationship is to learn to communicate in loving ways.

Men and women perceive love differently, which is a common cause for many misunderstandings, frictions and split-ups. Sometimes, what may be love to one partner can seem an inconsideration to the other. For a relationship to work in more harmony, one must learn to recognise love in any way it is expressed by the other partner. Many people who have workaholic partners feel neglected or unloved to a certain extent. But could it be that in the workaholic's mind, toiling long hours is their own expression of love for their other half in creating stronger financial security for both? Good relationships are built on opening up to each other in a deeper way, on intimate talks and on trust.

Complete trust is a pivotal factor in any successful

relationship. Lack of trust destroys the very foundation of any kinship. It undermines the core ingredients of love, the intimacy, the closeness and the confidence. No wonder that infidelity is one of the most common reasons for divorce. Unfaithfulness is an extreme betrayal of someone's confidence. That is why it is so painful. A breach of trust is a breach of love. To avoid outside temptations that can threaten to ruin the relationship, we have to exercise self-discipline. We must show maturity. We must develop an inner commitment and a sense of respect for each other. If problems come up do not bottle up your grievances because they will only fester and explode when least expected. Instead, diffuse the situation by talking about it frankly and lovingly with your partner. In this way, you truly extend yourself for nurturing the growth of both your partner and yourself.

Many people still marry for the wrong reasons. People will marry for money, to become socially comfortable, to get away from parents or out of sheer loneliness. Then there are those women who will rush to marry indiscriminately, because they reached an advanced age in which they are thinking in panic that the clock is ticking faster, or because they want children when it is still possible.

When two people feel an intense physical attraction, such as when they are sexually drawn to each other, they can mislead themselves into believing that they are in love; that they can start a relationship that will work. It seldom does. People who meet just for sex, however good the sex is, have nothing more than a sexual liaison. Sex alone cannot form a relationship. Sex is only one physical factor among several other emotional and mental elements which are needed as a foundation for a fulfilling relationship.

One can argue that no specific rules can guarantee a successful outcome in choosing Mr Right or Miss Right for a perfect relationship. True. Life is complex. Sometimes people may make a seemingly irrational decision, like marrying someone from a different culture or from a different age group, which may seem to be against all odds, yet still manage to create a rewarding and harmonious relationship. But these cases are few. It is like crossing a red traffic light in your car. You might manage to cross it with impunity, but at the cost of an increased risk. You have compounded your chances of getting involved in a collision. It is the same when choosing a partner. When you ignore the red lights of your common sense and intuition, you lower the chances of success. If you are baffled, ask yourself why and how in terms of your situation. *Framing the question is half the answer.* In a contemplative state, calm your mind chatter, relax and listen to your inner voice. Wait until you get an answer or an urge to take a course of action that feels positively good. It is always a good idea not to make rash decisions on the most important issues of your life.

If you want a marriage to have a fair chance of success, it is not a good idea to marry out of solitude. Not all people in this world are meant to be married. Some single people are so set in their ways that any attempt to cohabit with another person may be futile. Many people can evolve better through a solitary lifestyle. We each grow along a different pathway.

Do not think that being single discredits you. Most people have sometimes to go through a phase of solitude. As uncomfortable as this can be, living on your own even for a while offers an opportunity to discover your uniqueness. There is only one of you. When God created you, as one humorist said, He threw away the formula. Spending time alone can help you get to know yourself on a deeper level and enhance your self-love and self-acceptance. Use this time alone to meditate, to contemplate about the meaning of life and to learn to go with the flow. You can begin by striving to dissolve your resistances to any predicaments that you find disagreeable or unfair. Reflect on your connection to the power that created you and devised the script of your life. By developing an inner connection to spirit, you can be alone but not lonely.

By learning to enjoy your own company you are actually practising self-love. Treat yourself to a dinner and a show. Pamper yourself. Go on holiday. You can banish loneliness altogether when you learn to become your own best friend.

Loneliness is the inability to open up and share intimate feelings with another person. That is why a person can be lonely even when married. In long-standing dysfunctional marriages that lost their sparkle, partners can grow apart from each other. They can live their lives separately under the same roof, sharing the same house like roommates. Although they may do so allegedly out of habit or economical convenience, even if they have become alienated, more often than not, incompatible partners keep clinging to each other, putting up with the daily miseries of a hollow relationship, simply because they are afraid of being alone.

Self-love is an essential prerequisite *before* attempting a relationship. The first and foremost relationship you can ever have is with yourself. If you do not love yourself, if you do not accept yourself unconditionally and if you do not forgive yourself for your flaws, you will find it hard to love, accept and forgive another. If you do not live in peace with yourself, how can you live in peace with another human being? If you criticise yourself you will criticise your partner too. If you cannot accept people for who they are but only for who you want them to be, you are headed for disappointment.

If you do not really love yourself, no matter what your partner does, no matter how much he or she goes out of the way to please you, it will not be good enough. If you are self-loathing or insecure, if you deem yourself to be unworthy or insignificant, you will not feel you deserve this love and will not accept it. Without a measure of self-love, your partner will never be able to satisfy you because his or her words of affection will fall on deaf ears. You will not know how to accept and appreciate your partner's love, and you will find it even harder to reciprocate this love.

Actually, without adequate self-love it is difficult even to attract a successful relationship. Since all your relationships, in one way or another, mirror the one you have with yourself, it is obvious that you must first learn to love yourself before starting to go out looking for the perfect partner. An analogous situation is that any woman who wants a child should start a regime of balanced diet and supplementation *before* conception, in order to maximise the likelihood of a successful pregnancy and delivery.

Ideally, you should love yourself so much that you will hardly need a relationship to keep you happy. We need to realise that we want an intimate relationship with another person not because we lack love, but because we want to expand our love and grow to higher levels of happiness, fulfilment and enlightenment. In *Love and Survival – The Scientific Basis for the Healing Power of Intimacy*, Dr Dean Ornish says that finding his own health 'was not about finding the right person, but by being the right person'.

Jealousy can wreck any relationship. Are you or your partner overly jealous? Jealousy signifies a low sense of self-worth and a fragile personality. It is a reflection of insecurity and fear, emotions that are the opposite of love. If you or your partner are obsessively jealous people, you are undermining your love for each other. You are not yet ready for a truly fulfilling relationship. Start getting your emotional affairs in order. Work on your relationship with yourself. Embark on a self-discovery mission. Use any way you can think of to develop self-confidence and self-worth. Join a support group. Enrol in a growth workshop or see a therapist if you feel you need more personal help. Strengthen your inner connection with your higher self, train yourself to trust life. Sell yourself the idea that everything that happens to you has been perfectly designed for your higher good by a benevolent intelligence that is leading you to higher levels of love and fulfilment, regardless of what you are going through. Do not resist unavoidable, upsetting situations, because they constitute the flow of your life. They are your growth lessons. Endeavour to surrender and trust.

Love cannot live under domination. When one of the partners is an unhappy individual who is tormented by an inferiority complex, the relationship can become sour. To compensate for their own inadequacies, such people either try to dominate and control their partner, or alternatively, become submissive and compliant. They will either act in a condescending way or in a subservient way. These are two sides of the same coin. If you feel that your partner is walking all over you, remember that you cannot be trodden on unless you choose to lie down.

You have to realise that you are a whole person. If you feel that you need your other half to complete you, you are headed for a disappointment. As Dr Wayne Dyer, the noted psychologist, once said, 'In any relationship in which two people become one, the end result is two half people.' You must feel that you already have all the love you need within your own heart. You must feel naturally lovable. Let go of any disparaging thoughts. Strive to evolve your belief in your divine identity. You must upgrade your concepts to realise that you are a whole human being in your own right.

Love involves both union and separation. Although two persons may well unite their lives in the most intimate way, even to the point of becoming seemingly inseparable, they still retain their individuality. Each has his or her own uniqueness, idiosyncrasies, abilities and aspirations. They must both have their space within the relationship to pursue their unique purpose or they will feel stifled. Actually, it is the separateness of the partners that enriches the union. When we genuinely love our partners, we not only respect their individuality; we lovingly extend ourselves to support them in whatever ambition they are pursuing, even if it may seem that this might draw us apart. Know that the more freedom and support you give your partner, the more likely he or she will be attracted to you. Dare to take the leap of faith. Trust that whatever you invest in the growth of your partner you will reap in even greater growth of your own spirit. It is the law of cause and effect in action.

Expressing his views on union and separation in marriage, Kahlil Gibran wrote in *The Prophet*:

But let there be spaces in your togetherness,
And let the winds of heavens dance between you.

Love one another, but make not a bond of love;
Let it rather be a moving sea between the shores of
  your souls.
Fill each other's cup but drink not from one cup.
Give one another of your bread but eat not from the
  same loaf,
Sing and dance together and be joyous, but let each
  one
Of you be alone,
Even as the strings of a lute are alone though they
Quiver with the same music.

Give your hearts, but not into each other's keeping.
For only the hand of Life can contain your hearts.
And stand together yet not too near together:
For the pillars of the temple stand apart,
And the oak tree and the cypress grow not in each
  other's shadow.

Falling in love is a distinct state of mind of two people whose mental boundaries have collapsed. They merge together in ecstasy as if they have temporarily lost their identity. For a while they become one. They feel a huge surge of power which deludes them into believing that they can overcome all problems. But this unrealistic feeling is a misconception. First, because falling in love is primarily a sex-motivated experience. You do not fall in love with your children although you love them very much. Second, since in most cases this is an irrational fantasy, it is temporary. Just as we can fall in love, we can also fall out of love, whether or not the relationship survives its initial phase and becomes long-term. If it does become long-term, the partners will not stop loving each other, but the ecstasy will gradually die out. The reality of daily life will open their eyes and reveal their different personalities. Eventually, they will come to respect each other's individuality. Actually, it is only when a couple fall out of their euphoric love and lose their initial ecstasy that they can begin to experience real kinship, in a mature and lasting love.

In long-term loving relationships, however, the gaps between partners become gradually smaller to a certain extent, as partners tend to adjust and affect each other's way of thinking and daily habits. We unwittingly pick from each other new mannerisms, new concepts and new modes of behaviour. We must be alert to pick only the higher traits that can serve our growth, and disregard the lower ones.

Over many years of togetherness, some roles played by one partner may be reciprocated by the other. Partners become, in a way, more coordinated, more aligned and more harmonious. We can often see this in an old couple taking a leisurely stroll in the park; they seem to walk in identical footsteps and at an even pace, much like well-trained soldiers in a military parade. That is fine. They are not encroaching on each other's territory. It is a mutual voluntary adaptation, adjustment and growth. This is how a relationship can be elevated to a higher level of harmony and love.

9

Living with Joy

Happiness is our divine legacy. But we have to claim it to have it. We have to choose the path of joy, simply determine to be happy. Joy is an inside job. It arises from within our thinking patterns, not from outer circumstances. Actually, *happiness is an attitude of mind.* Abraham Lincoln said that people are just about as happy as they make up their minds to be. On the path of growth, joy is a major priority. Two thousand years ago the Roman philosopher and stoic Seneca said, 'Before all else, learn how to feel joy.' Happiness is a part of the Higher Will since it is the nature of the soul to exist in a state of bliss. To be happy, we simply need to reconnect with our divine nature.

You cannot plan, arrange or organise to be happy because happiness is a mental attitude. The pursuit of happiness as an independent goal never works because it is based on the misconception that happiness is outside us. We may strive but never arrive, since real happiness is from within. Even a holiday cruise on a luxurious liner to a five-star Caribbean resort cannot make you happy if you are ravaged by fears and worries, because you will be taking all your distressing anxieties with you. Happiness can only be experienced as a by-product of other pursuits, such as the pursuit of love, the pursuit of oneness with life and an expansion of generous endeavours. An ongoing practice of helping people in need creates inner satisfying happiness.

Dr Albert Schweitzer, the great surgeon, philosopher and Bible scholar who devoted his life to bringing health and education to natives of equatorial Africa, was a most happy man. He said, 'In happiness to others you know happiness.' If you want to be happy, make others happy. And much like self-love, happiness is not a destination, it is a way of life.

Peak experiences, a term first coined by the American psychologist Abraham Maslow, describes surges of exhilarating moments when suddenly, out of the blue, we are catapulted beyond the confines of the mundane and the ordinary, such as when we experience a stunningly colourful sunset, a shimmering lake in the morning sun, or a breathtaking scenic landscape from a mountain top that leaves us in a full awe. Such a peak experience is a kind of 'peek experience', because this is when we catch a glimpse of the blissful state of our soul, and for a brief moment we actually become one with our higher self. This is when our divine bliss shines through. This is when we mostly feel at one with divinity. Maslow discovered that the more peaks you have, the more content, happy and successful you are likely to be. The first step to create more peaks is to make a decision. You decide to see beauty and loveliness in people and things around you. You train yourself to look at life through rose-coloured glasses. You become oblivious to ugliness. The more you practise, the better you get, and therefore the more inclined to attract those rare experiences that the mystics call 'heaven on earth'.

Falling in love with life is a way towards a blissful existence. Imagine that 'the one and only' came into your life. What a euphoric feeling it stirs up. When you fall in love for the first time you do not see any faults in your beloved. It feels as if he or she is perfect. It seems the whole world is perfect and problems are a mere triviality. You are on cloud nine. You love the mundane and the spiritual, the virtuous and the sinner alike. Know that you can develop the same emotional intoxication with life, and as you do, you are more likely to come across occasional peak experiences.

To feel worthy of happiness you must learn to love yourself more. As you do, you also realise that you are lovable. Indeed you are loved by life more than you know. In the words of Victor Hugo, 'The supreme happiness of life is the conviction that we are loved.'

In fact, divine bliss is our inner essence; it is who we really are. Our core is a focus of everlasting joy. A passage in *A Course in Miracles* states: 'It is hard to understand what "The Kingdom of Heaven is Within you" really means. This is because it is not understandable to the ego, which interprets it as if something outside is inside, and this does not mean anything. The word "within" is unnecessary. The kingdom of heaven is you.'

To get closer to a state of true and lasting happiness, we have to go inward and reconnect ourselves to our higher self, the source of joy which always exists within us. True happiness is natural, abundant and always available. It is usually only with time, as we grow wiser, that we realise in hindsight that materialism in itself cannot bring happiness. Achievements, successes and windfalls can only encourage and bolster our happiness, not create it.

Happiness can be very confusing. In our materialistic society people are conditioned to think of career advancements and financial success as synonymous with happiness. For most people winning the lottery is the ultimate bliss. Workaholics struggle and strive to attain relationship X, income level Y or social status Z, only to discover that getting it did not bring them the lasting happiness they expected. True joy transpires from the capability to see that there is more to life than financial success.

Many people who fail to achieve what seems to be a

satisfying loving and harmonious relationship sadly feel that happiness has eluded them. This can make people cynical and confused about the whole idea of happiness. Filmmaker Woody Allen describes this contradiction in his typical twisted humour: 'To love is to suffer. To avoid suffering one must not love, but then one suffers from not loving. Therefore, to love is to suffer, not to love is to suffer, to suffer is to suffer. To be happy is to love. To be happy then is to suffer. But suffering makes one unhappy. Therefore, to be unhappy one must love or love to suffer. Or suffer from too much happiness.'

Happiness erroneously seems to depend on whether we get what we wish for. That is why we often get frustrated when our goals don't turn out as we desire. Happiness, however, is a personal choice, a conscious decision to be happy regardless, not something which depends on a certain outside occurrence. We experience pain only when we choose to make our happiness dependent on something we cannot control.

In the twenty-first century, we live in a society of affluence without any parallel to the past. Royalties of bygone eras could not even dream about luxuries now taken for granted by the masses, like air travel, television, Internet, satellite navigation and air-conditioning. Did all this help to make us joyful? Are we now happier than previous generations? Judging by the massive sales of anti-depressants and tranquillisers such as Prozac, it seems like the opposite is the case. In a study entitled *The Pursuit of Happiness – Discovering the Pathway to Fulfilment, Well-being, and Enduring Personal Joy*, social psychologist Dr David Myers sums the situation up:

'. . . whether we base our conclusions on self-reported happiness, rates of depression, or teen problems, our becoming better-off over the last thirty years has not been accompanied by one iota of increased happiness and life satisfaction. It's shocking, because it contradicts our society's materialistic assumptions, but how can we ignore the hard truth: Once beyond poverty, further economic growth does not appreciably improve human morale. Making more money – the aim of so many graduates and other American dreamers of the 1980's – does not breed bliss.'

Money cannot buy happiness because happiness is not in what we physically have, it is in what we mentally are. You do not need to have a million dollars to feel like a million dollars.

Always look on the bright side of life. Train your mind to think in an optimistic way, and according to the law of attraction, you will tend to attract more optimistic outcomes in your affairs. A recent statistical study showed that on average, optimists live seven years longer than the average life-span. In fact, if you keep worrying about the undesirable, your worries will spread also to favourable issues that you are happy about, and adversely affect them. To highlight the positive, start by counting your blessings daily. This can help you feel appreciative and cheerful. And the more cheerful you are, the more you create events to be cheerful about. To put your problems in a proper perspective, lend an ear to other people's tragic woes. Sympathetic listening is not only a service to others, it is also a service to yourself; it helps you realise how small your own problems are in comparison and how much you have to be grateful for.

The ability to live in the here and now can help you keep happy. Condition your mind to think that you only live in 'today' units of time because that is really where you actually live. 'Now' is the only reality. Yesterday and tomorrow are not realities; they are only figments of your imagination. You may feel dispirited when you mentally try to relive former disappointments or become worried trying to imagine the uncertain future. But low spirits are a recipe for dissatisfaction, just as happy feelings are a promise of gratification. So dwell on the happiness of your present moment. When the Dalai Lama was once asked when the happiest time in his life was, he promptly replied: 'Right now.'

The key to staying in the here and now is to suspend judgement and prediction. When you judge, you are relating to the past. When you predict, you are relating to the future. You can brush aside past blunders when you realise that they cannot be changed. You can dismiss the worries for tomorrow when you train yourself to trust in the benevolence of the universe, when you develop an unshakeable belief that the same power who kept you so far will keep on sustaining you. And never look back in anger, shame or guilt, because you do not want to attract more of the same. Release yesterday's setbacks with love because they were intended as necessary lessons on your growth path. It is these past experiences that brought you to your wiser present. Remember how ephemeral and fleeting is your day so try to make the most of it. Do not let your past cripple your present.

Remember that:

> The present is just a moment in time,
> Gone by the time you finish this line.
> What you just read is in the past,
> So treasure each moment, as if it's the last.

Many of us create our own unhappiness by constantly worrying about our problems and adversities. It seems more 'practical' to dwell on our misfortunes than to reflect on our blessings. So many unhappy people keep replaying unfortunate scenarios in their minds over and over again, without realising that they are using the law of attraction to their detriment. But there is a better way. Stop focusing on your problem. Instead, shift your attention to your desired outcome and let the law of attraction attract a solution. By playing out the fears of the ego, you are perpetuating your unhappiness. You are acting as your own worst enemy. You need to simply love yourself more in order to feel worthy of your God-given happiness. You have to accept joy as your natural birthright.

Imagine getting so deeply into a soap opera that you can't sleep for worrying how things will turn out! In the soap opera of daily life, though, we all get more hooked that we ought. We fret about events we cannot influence. We waste energy trying to turn back tides. We don't place enough faith in divine providence and serendipity. The truth is that there are some situations we can have a positive impact on, and some that are better left alone to sort themselves out. We must be aware to know which is which.

Worry is a common futile affliction which serves only to ruin our peace of mind. It was Mark Twain who remarked in hindsight, 'The worst troubles I've had in my life are the ones that never happened.' To be happy, one must break the worry habit. If spontaneous worries are torturing you, remind yourself that you are not a helpless victim of your thoughts. You are in charge of your mind and can choose what to think. So assume control over your thoughts. Be vigilant. When a worrying thought comes along, substitute it immediately with an optimistic one. Remind yourself that your pressing predicament has a reason and a message designed for your higher good by a loving intelligence. Positive thoughts are highly powerful; one positive thought can cancel out hundreds of negative ones. Practising faith attitudes takes time and effort, but with determination and perseverance, you will eventually have trained your mind to think optimistically and draw the happy events to you that you so desire.

To put gloominess out of life why not be a Pollyanna? In this classic book and Disney movie, Pollyana is a girl who manages to keep doom and gloom at bay by finding something to be glad about in every situation. A former work-mate of mine woke up one morning to find that his car was jacked up, perched on piles of bricks, and the four wheels were gone. Imagine the initial shock. However, as he was relating the incident to his colleagues, he said jubilantly, 'Although the thieves took the wheels they did leave all the wheel nuts under the car. I can easily buy new wheels, but do you know how hard it is to find matching nuts for my old car?' Practising a Pollyanna attitude can help build a cheerful consciousness of optimism and confidence.

True happiness is unconditional. It is a feeling of inner joy which must not be allowed to be affected by adversities, setbacks or trying situations. A story in *Lessons of St Francis of Assisi* by John Talbot beautifully illustrates this. When St Francis was asked by Brother Leo, 'What is perfect joy?' he replied with the following story: 'Imagine that I return to Perugia on the darkest of nights, a night so cold that everything is covered with snow, and the frost in the folds of my habit hits my legs and makes them bleed. Shrouded in snow and shivering with cold, I arrive at the door of the friary, and after calling out for a long time, the Brother porter gets up and asks: "Who is it?" And I respond: "It is I, Brother Francis." The porter says: "Be on your way. Now is not the time to arrive at the friary. I will not open the door for you." I insist and he answers: "Be on your way right now. You are stupid and an idiot. We are already many here and we do not need you." I insist once more: "For the love of God, let me in, just for tonight." And he answers: "Not even to talk. Go to the leper colony that is nearby." Well, Brother Leo, if after all this I do not lose patience and remain calm, believe me, that is perfect joy.'

Henry Bolingbroke, the seventeenth-century statesman, wrote, 'He alone is happy and he is truly so, who can say, "Welcome life, whatever it brings! Welcome death whatever it is."' Learning to trust life and flow with whatever it brings takes time. That is why people tend to mature and get happier with time. They have learned to take unexpected problems with a pinch of salt. They do not allow troubles to disturb them. Nowadays, youth is greatly overrated, as if being young is a passport to joy and delight. Young people, however, have relatively less money, work the hardest of anyone, are neurotic about their appearance and most important, are unsure about their identity and future.

Over the years, though, as young people with open minds grow older in the school of life, their outstanding issues have been resolved one way or another. They tend to come to terms with their lives, whether they achieved whatever they set out to accomplish or not. They become more refined in character and demeanour. They are happier because they have learned to appreciate their blessings, rather than take them for granted. They have gained a certain level of trust and are less bothered by insignificant issues. In hindsight, they start to realise that life is working with them, not against them. As Nachman Meouman, the eighteenth-century mystic rabbi, said, 'When a man knows that all his life events are for his own good, this realization in itself is a kind of heavenly bliss.' Middle-aged people have a greater tendency to look beyond the physical. They are more inclined to see the joys and sorrows of life from a higher perspective. They can better identify with the words of Kahlil Gibran: 'Your joy is your sorrow unmasked.'

In the United Kingdom, where it frequently rains more than it shines, it is not uncommon to wake up in the morning, turn on the TV and hear the day's weather forecast as 'grey and dull'. What a way to start a day! Is it any wonder that many people commuting to work in the morning wear such long and glum faces?

When on one overcast morning someone was trying to share his morning gloom with me, I remarked: 'I prefer the biblical message. The Bible says: "This is the day the Lord has made; we will rejoice and be glad in it" [Psalms 118:24]. Did the Bible say, this cloudy day, this rainy day or this sunny day? It did not specify. Every day is a gift. So rise and shine! Do not rise and whine. Greet every new day with a smile. Waking up alive is reason enough to be happy. Release your inner joy. By dwelling on positive ideas and optimistic intentions you start to put your thoughts on a joyful slant. You create a happy attitude of mind regardless of any weather conditions.' Remember: the weather is beyond your control. Your mood is not.

The media contributes a significant share to public misery by concentrating its attention on disastrous news. Good tidings do not seem to make much impact, but misfortunes and crimes always make headlines. Can you remember when you have last seen a piece of good and uplifting news in the papers or on the TV? One day, while buying my evening paper, I asked my local newsagent in jest, 'Any good news today?' He answered, 'Good news don't sell newspapers.'

Complaining breeds unhappiness. It implies resistance to the flow of life. Eventually, complaints are a killjoy. To build a strong and happy character, it helps to make yourself a positive set of rules to strive to live by. Many great personalities have done this. The late movie star Katharine Hepburn, who died at the ripe old age of 96, had a simple set of rules: 'Never complain. Don't brag. Seek challenges. Never give up.'

We often make ourselves unhappy by comparing our status, income or success with other people, especially colleagues and competitors. We forget that we are unique, valuable and incomparable. We need to be constantly reminded of the great truth – that each life is an individual experience. Comparisons are futile; they only lead to jealousy, rivalry and unhappiness. They ruin our peace of mind. To feel happy, appreciate what you have. *Ethics of the*

Fathers, the book of ancient Jewish wisdom, states: 'Rich is he who is content in his lot.' Of course. If you are not content with what you have, how can you be happy? Riches do not guarantee happiness. A person can have millions and still feel inadequate and miserable. Contentment, however, does not mean ceasing to aspire to higher achievements or bigger accomplishments. It just means that you choose to be content with what you have right now. Practising contentment leads to equanimity and serenity, the antidotes of greed and jealousy, two of the greatest pitfalls to happiness.

Often the greatest sense of happiness comes from the knowledge that you are not alone in this world. This feeling evolves gradually as you develop a strong inner connection with your spirit, usually through meditation. You come to realise that a higher force for good is running your life. You get a notion that come rain or shine, you will always be looked after, and that one way or another, you will always manage. You come to trust that you are sustained by a loving presence; that your creator is your loyal and loving ally who will never fail you nor forsake you; that your needs will always be met and when you ask for help or guidance, you will get it. The universe will send you ideas; doors will open; people will reach out with money, love and support. With time, you come to feel that the universe, the power of all creation, God or whatever name you prefer to call it, is your divine partner with whom you can share your difficulties and to whom you can talk any time. You diminish the fears that plague our society; you abate the anxieties that ruin the happiness of so many people. You gradually realise that you are indeed totally safe and protected, guided and loved by a higher power. You are definitely not alone.

Reaching this awareness is an important milestone in your growth path. It leads you to feel an unshakeable confidence. You get the feeling that whatever is happening to you right now is actually preparing you for more and better, even if you cannot understand how or why. You come to believe that an unseen intelligence makes everything happen for your higher good. You can thus transcend loneliness, and strike a relationship with your higher self, your divine link for sustaining happiness.

Knowing that you are a co-creator with the universe is another is another great source of inner joy. When the Bible says, 'The Lord is the strength of my life,' it is actually saying that you have within you an infinite power to overcome all odds. It further means that you have a share of God's infinite potential for creativity. You can have whatever you want as long as it is for your higher good. And what if you do not know what your higher good is? Don't worry. Just remember the age-old expression, 'God is good and wise in what He gives and what He denies.' Realise that if your goal is for your higher good, it will come at the right time, when you are ready for it. The universe will not deprive you of anything that serves your spiritual growth and your higher good. And that is reason enough to be happy.

Have you noticed that when you are happy you feel powerful and inspired and when downtrodden you feel apathetic and helpless? That is because joy is a life charger whereas gloominess is a life drainer. According to the Kabbalah, joy or 'Chayoot' is life energy, much like the Chinese concept of *chi*. Kabbalists teach that joy is both the source and the channel of spiritual energy and when you decide to be happy you become a conduit of divine power. That is why a person on cloud nine feels so powerful and so full of life. As an Old Testament verse of King Solomon goes, 'Gladness of heart is life to a man.'

Unconditional self-acceptance is a key to a lasting happiness. When you lovingly accept yourself as you are, there is no need to pacify self-imposed preconditions like 'should' or 'must' that cause inner conflicts, such as, 'I must lose

140

weight,' 'I must gain weight,' 'I should jog every morning,' or 'I must get that promotion.' True happiness is an unconditional emotion that does not depend on your successes or failures. Happiness is being in congruence with yourself in the here and now rather than berating yourself for lack of nerve or will power. Once you calm down and acknowledge your power, you stop the inner war. You can then relax and let your inner wisdom guide you in the best way that suits you to materialise your aspirations.

The continuous practice of self-acceptance leads to peace and happiness. Without self-acceptance nothing is enough; with self-acceptance, you are enough. The following story I heard as a teenager illustrates this. Jack was fishing by the river on a hot summer day as a well-dressed stranger came along and asked, 'Catch any trout today?' Jack replied, 'Yes, I caught about a dozen but I threw them back in the water.' The stranger exclaimed, 'What? Twelve fish and you did not sell them? Why, you could have made a nice profit!' 'And then what?' asked Jack. 'Well,' said the stranger, 'you could then buy yourself a better rod and catch more fish.' 'Why would I want more fish?' asked Jack. The stranger explained, 'More fish means more profit and with more money you could buy a van and sell even more fish.' 'But I enjoy it here just being happy,' said Jack. Disregarding this, the stranger continued, 'OK, but with more money you could start a fish restaurant and if you work hard enough, you could end up owning a chain of restaurants and become rich.' 'So what if I do?' asked Jack. 'Well,' said the stranger, 'when you are rich enough, you can do what you want. You can come here anytime you like and fish for pleasure.' 'Isn't that what I am already doing right now?' asked Jack. In this story, leisure fishing symbolises our happy higher self, while the stranger represents our fearful ego, this nagging urge which is always trying to tell us that happiness is conditional and depends on material conditions.

Merging with the oneness of humanity increases our sense of happiness. To develop our sense of universal unity, we must give up our tendency to affix labels saying 'good' or 'bad' to people and situations, because this promotes separateness. My grandmother, a woman of great traditional wisdom, used to say, 'Everything is an idea.' Whether a person or a situation is good or bad, hard or easy, pleasant or unpleasant is only a notion in the mind. We are not doomed to put up with distressing ideas; we can substitute them with happier ones. It only takes a choice. Just as you can think yourself to unhappiness and failure, so can you think yourself to happiness and success. As soon as you make it a habit to think positively, you begin to change your life for the better. William James, the famous American psychologist and thinker, said, 'The greatest discovery of my generation is that human beings can alter their lives by altering their attitudes of mind.' As you think, so shall you be. So flush out old tired thoughts of doom and gloom. Fill your mind with fresh thoughts of love, faith and optimism and enjoy a happier life. It only takes a decision.

Acts of love purify the personality, and purity of character promotes inner happiness. When you speak from the heart, you make a loving and gratifying connection. Good intentions and selfless acts of kindness make you happy; plotting and wrongdoing make you unhappy. You cannot know happiness when you abuse people, when you are harsh, arrogant or inconsiderate. Refining the ego creates inner peace, and inner peace is the birthplace of happiness from which the latter grows and expands. A person with a tamed ego has the ability to get along with other people in loving ways, without judgement or criticism, and to assist them to recognise their own divinity.

When differences of opinion occur in a relationship, you have to choose between being right or being happy. Getting into a power struggle over control, over an opinion or for proving someone's guilt ruins happiness. That is when people attack, defend, get hurt, get petty, become resentful and conceited. If you feel you are right, you can argue your point at the expense of your happiness. Didn't you know that the best way to win an argument is not to argue?

Much like chemical addictions, mental addictions which are stimulated by the ego rob us of our happiness. According to the late Ken Keyes Jr., author of *Handbook to Higher Consciousness*, we have to free ourselves from security, sensation and power addictions before we can rise to experience happiness. When we are addicted to security, we cannot get 'enough' in material terms to feel secure. With an addiction to sensual pleasures, we cannot get enough sex to be satisfied. And when addicted to power, we bully, dominate and manipulate people and situations to boost our prestige, wealth and pride because we believe that 'might makes right'. These addictions are tormenting and insatiable and are hard to overcome by sheer will power. Instead, by striving to evolve spiritually, addictions can be raised to higher levels of conscious-awareness.

Addictions cease to torment us when they become preferences. We now *prefer* the things that we previously craved. Now, we do not need to have them at any cost in order to be happy. There are no withdrawal symptoms of dissatisfaction any more. Our happiness is no longer conditional. As Ken Keyes Jr. said, 'Happiness happens when your consciousness is not dominated by addictions and demands, and you experience life as a parade of preferences.'

Likewise, attachments are a common cause of emotional pain. People tend to cling to what they have – a job, a relationship or a habit – because they reckon that this may be the best they can get. When the winds of change start blowing, as familiar life structures are crumbling, many people become fearful. Something seems to be leaving their lives but they just won't let go; they resist change at all costs. Attachments are a source of needless suffering and letting go of them is a gateway to happiness. Non-attachment is an aspect of trust in the all-loving nature of the universe that constantly sustains life. Keep saying to yourself that life is perfect and everything that happens is perfect. In times of change learn to trust your intuitive messages. Many people do not realise the great truth – that nothing is ever taken away unless something better is on its way. The more easily you let go of the old and open up for the new, the more you can grow through joy.

Happiness often eludes us when we do not follow our soul's calling, our vocation in life. We may get inner urges to capitalise on a talent we feel attracted to, but suppress it because it seems difficult, near impossible, even 'crazy'. You may be dreaming of starting an organic farm while you are stuck in an office job you feel you depend on. When we do not summon the courage to follow our natural inclination, be it climbing mountains, playing the piano or taking flying lessons, a feeling of inner dissatisfaction keeps eroding our happiness. You may be a middle-aged person who says, 'I always liked to paint but how can I quit a job that secures my livelihood?' This nagging urge will always prevent you from feeling fulfilled until you decide to do something about it. You will have to face your fears and figure out ways to overcome obstacles on the way to pursuing your God-given vocation. Happiness comes from your enjoyment of doing the things you were meant to do in this lifetime.

The ultimate way to happiness is unconditional love. Love transcends all negativity. Love condones any offence. Unconditional love is the great promise of joy. Open your heart to love and you will be happy. A passage in *A Course in Miracles* reads, 'Whenever you are not wholly joyous it is because you have reacted with lack of love to one of God's creation.'

144

Self-love is pivotal. Eventually, it is the level of your self-love that determines how you treat yourself and how the whole world treats you. No one will love you more than you love yourself. Happiness is a natural consequence of self-love. True happiness can only be experienced when we love ourselves unconditionally; when our love has grown to higher levels of consciousness.

10

Claim Your Power

Deep within man dwell those slumbering powers;
powers that would astonish him,
that he never dreamed of possessing;
forces that would revolutionise his life
if aroused and put to action.

(Orison Swett Marden)

There is a huge creative power of infinite intelligence operating within each human being. Each person is a distinct focus of divine power and yet so many of us feel powerless in various life situations. Many people commonly feel that human beings are helpless pawns in a higher scheme of whimsical fate, like a rowing boat deprived of oars and rudder, drifting aimlessly on a vast ocean at the total mercy of unpredictable weather conditions. They feel doomed to struggle against poor odds and often tend to expect the worst outcome. In a sense this is understandable. When we feel alone in this world, unaware of our God-given power, we can indeed feel helpless. It is only when we open up to realise that we are actually a channel for a higher power which is constantly leading us to a higher purpose that we become powerful. People who do not believe that they possess this inner power are people who have not yet discovered their divine identity.

For thousands of years the Bible has taught that 'the kingdom of God is within you'. What is this kingdom and where does it reside? This kingdom is a divine potency of infinite wisdom and creativity. This supreme power resides in our unconscious mind, a mental faculty we are not conscious of, which makes up 95 per cent of our brain, whereas only 5 per cent of the brain comprises our conscious mind, the mind we commonly use to think, to reason and to analyse. The unconscious mind is our divine kingdom. It is the realm of higher dimensions, the seat of our sixth sense. It is the source of intuition, gut feelings and insights, where everything is possible and where miracles are produced easily and effortlessly. How then can we access this elusive power and how do we harness its powers to work for us?

The unconscious mind is constantly and automatically influenced by what we think consciously, by our feelings, desires and expectations. It is activated by our imagination and mostly by our convictions, by what we believe is true for us. It is, however, a neutral power, which, like a computer, will create whatever our conscious thinking, as a keyboard, programmes into it. That is why it is vitally important to think positively and optimistically. We can give this limitless power any direction we want just by developing a strong desire for any specific goal, from healing a disease to creating prosperity. We can really conceive of this power as a wish-granting genie!

It is important, however, to realise that the power will grant us only those wants which conform to our core beliefs. If we think of something we desire, but deep down we do not feel worthy of it or doubt that it is at all possible because we cannot see where it is coming from, as in wishful thinking, the whole idea will remain a wishful thought. As the Bible promises, God will 'grant thee according to thine own heart' (Psalms 20:4). To make our want a physical reality, we must bring ourselves to desire it with all our heart, without a shadow of doubt. We must desire it so intensely, so fiercely, that we feel we cannot live without it. We thus condition our unconscious mind, trusting in its power to provide it. Our mere faith in our goal will magnetise it to us. Belief is the greatest booster of creative power. To use our power efficiently, we must first know exactly what we want and then trust our power implicitly. We must believe in belief, because belief is the law of creativity. It is in fact the law of life.

The most common pitfall in the use of the power is when our blind trust gets eroded by the doubts of our rational mind that tells us to be realistic and not get carried away by some far-fetched fantasy. Sometimes when we embark on a venture to achieve an important goal, we are pestered by worries about the outcome of the endeavour. You must keep mentally alert. You must learn to discipline your mind. Where before you could think indiscriminately, you now train yourself to reject the old might-not-get ideas from your thinking. Any time a negative thought comes to mind, cancel it out with a positive one. Insist on being optimistic! Learn to suspend disbelief. It is well worth the effort because by worrying, you are actually attracting that which you are worrying about.

Suppose you want a bigger house but have no savings and cannot afford a bigger mortgage on your present earnings. You cannot, for the life of you, figure out how you can make it happen. However, once you firmly decide to have it, you set in motion unforeseen factors. Constantly visualise your new house in every detail. Feel the joy of living in it in your heart. Keep your faith for as long as it takes and then watch the power of your unconscious manifest it for you in ways you could have never thought out with your tiny rational mind.

Imagination and visualisation are most powerful tools to

materialise any desire. Visualise and fantasise frequently. While visualising, however, feel that your desires are met. Feel the thrill of enjoying them as if you had them now. A joyous feeling of expectancy is highly important in unleashing your inner power.

A woman living with her husband on a meagre income wanted a piano. Having heard about the power of creative visualisation, she decided to put it to the test. She did not ask for money to buy it because she knew her husband would use the money for more basic needs. She started visualising a piano in her living room. She moved some furniture to make space for it and every day when she dusted the furniture, she would pretend to dust her imaginary piano. She started to gradually feel the excitement of having it. She did not care whether she was being realistic. Nor did she allow her doubts to creep in. To her, the piano would drop from the sky any day now.

After a few weeks, she received a call from a salesman offering a special deal on a piano. She smiled but said she had no money. A couple of weeks later another piano dealer called, and the woman started to think that all these dealers calling her must be a sign that her fantasies were taking effect. She grew increasingly excited.

One day, she stood up in a crowded bus to give up her seat to an old lady. They got off together at the same stop but since they did not know each other, they did not speak. Suddenly, however, the old lady dropped her umbrella and the woman picked it up for her, and thus, they started talking. The old lady said, 'I don't suppose you happen to know someone who would store a piano? I have to travel abroad and I want someone to use it for three years, free of charge, instead of paying for storage.' The woman who was visualising the piano was spellbound. The power of visualisation had worked! She got herself a piano for three years. In hindsight, however, she realised that she could have had her own piano from the start, had her consciousness been bigger. She only conceived of the idea of storing someone's piano, and by the law of attraction that was what she attracted. Had she dared to think that there are many millions of pianos in the world and that one could be hers, she could easily have had one of her own. The piano woman, however, learned the lesson. She increased the size of her consciousness by increasing her ability to envision, and by the end of three years, when the old lady came to reclaim her piano, this woman had become rich enough to buy a piano by using the same power of visualisation. The power of our unconscious mind is unlimited. It is we who limit it by the size of our consciousness.

The concept of infinite power is not easily accepted by our mind. We were all brought up to think in finite terms; to set limits to our abilities. We were taught to think sensibly, and to realise that we cannot be childish and expect to create any goal we fancy. In our culture logic is eulogised as the ultimate wisdom and we are educated to accept its ruling of what is rationally possible versus what is irrationally impossible. However, as we evolve, we begin to discover the infinite wisdom of our intuitive power. Our rationale is a fine thing. We can use it to analyse conditions and possibilities and make informed choices. Intuition, however, does not care much about details. It either feels something or it does not. Little or no dialogue ensues between these two forces. Rationale dismisses intuition because intuition cannot be explained rationally. Intuition, on the other hand, plays down rationale because it thinks it knows it all. One true flash of emotional insight, however, is worth a million logical explanations.

After decades of finite thinking, a concept of infinite 'illogical' wisdom can feel strange and incomprehensible. But when we start to get it, we are led to overrule the limitations of our rationale. We are guided to believe that anything within the material plane is possible, and that we are only limited by the size of our imagination, by what we can accept as possible.

To set yourself on a path of self-discovery take a moment to relax and reflect. Where did you come from? Who or what created you? And for what purpose? These soul-searching questions are not necessarily intended to make you pursue the study of the mystical Kabbalah, which deals with these issues. However, by reflecting on these topics in a way the Buddhists call mindfulness, you may eventually come to realise that you are more than an isolated human entity. Just like the trees, the birds and the mountains, you are part of a limitless universe created and sustained by the infinite intelligence of life. As such, you are an integral part, an individualised focus of this infinite creative intelligence.

When we accept the idea that there is a higher creative wisdom within us which runs our life in ways we cannot understand, it is easier to accept our true identity as part of a greater wholeness. As children of God, we are each a prince or princess of the universe, but most of us do not realise it. We are all royalties of a boundless kingdom and yet we deceive ourselves to be commoners. We are reluctant to accept our divine identity. To quote the poet Emily Dickinson:

> We never know how high we are
> Till we are called to rise;
> And then, if we are true to plan,
> Our statures touch the skies.
> The heroism we recite
> Would be a daily thing,
> Did not ourselves the cubits warp
> For fear to be a king.

151

Since we have a source of infinite power and wisdom at our command we can have anything we want. We can use our inner wisdom to help us solve any problem and overcome any difficulty. All along history, we can read about people who were able to rise above 'impossible' situations and overcome seemingly insurmountable odds. Likewise, we can each work magic. All we have to do is focus our attention and mentally give our inner power a direction. Our higher wisdom then goes to create whatever it is we focus on in a magical way. We are not slaves to any uncontrollable, discouraging thoughts that happen to turn up. We have the power to monitor our thinking. We can choose the thoughts that lead us towards our goals just as a ship captain has the authority to choose the best course to his port of call.

If you need more proof that you are a channel for a higher intelligence, contemplate for a moment your physical existence. What is the invisible power that is keeping you alive and active? What is this infinite wisdom within you that orchestrates in perfect timing all the involuntary functions over which you have no direct control, such as your heartbeat and your metabolism? Think of the billions of biochemical reactions that happen every second in every cell, which are required to maintain your body in a balanced state of well-being. Do you know how to digest your food? How to heal your wounds? Or how to keep healthy in the midst of all the environmental pollutants to which you are constantly exposed? It takes the intricate intelligence of your immune system to identify and engulf hostile germs while sparing your friendly bacteria. Antioxidants from our diet are skilfully directed to intercept and inactivate free radicals, those destructive particles which attack our DNA and threaten to inflict upon us the degenerative diseases of ageing such as heart attacks, cancer and strokes. Our health is a miracle against seemingly insurmountable odds and yet most of us take it for granted! As you learn more about human anatomy and physiology, you come to realise that your body is run by a higher intelligence which is encoded in your genome, your genetic blueprint which holds the secrets of your life, far beyond your ability to control or understand, but well within your capability to trust and have faith in.

A burning desire or an intense ambition are powerful driving forces in the human mind. Faithful expectation is a dynamic magnetising energy. A person who expects success already tends to have success, just as one who considers failure tends to fail. Every thought has an impact. By simply holding a notion in mind we are influencing an event. By contemplating success or failure we set in motion energies that attract and materialise our specific thoughts. In a TV interview a self-made millionaire was asked to share his secret of success. His answer was: 'Always think you are lucky.' Becoming successful is just a matter of constant conditioning of the mind to believe in success. You do it by constantly substituting negative thoughts with positive ones.

There is an old sport story about the San Antonio club of the Texas league of baseball, which at one time had an assortment of great players, and everyone thought they would easily take the championship. However, the team fell into a slump and lost seventeen of its first twenty games. The players seemed hardly able to hit anything, and consequently started to accuse each other of jinxing the club. One day, after being badly beaten by a very poor team, the players became totally demoralised. Their manager Josh O'Reilly, however, knew that he had an array of star players and realised that they simply lost their faith in their ability. Instead of winning, they got on the pitch expecting to be defeated. This negative thinking froze their muscles and messed up their instincts and coordination.

At that time, a local preacher called Schlater was very

popular in this area as a faith healer and was reputed to achieve amazing healing results. O'Reilly asked each player to lend him his two best bats. He then put all the bats in a wheelbarrow, asked his players to wait and went off with the bats. He returned after an hour to tell the players that Schlater, the famous preacher, had blessed the bats and that these bats now contained a power which could not be defeated. The players were obviously delighted and elated. The next day, they overwhelmed the Dallas club. They triumphed their way into the championship and for years, rumour had it that a South West player would pay a large sum for a 'Schlater bat'. What really made the astonishing change was not Schlater's power. It was the renewed confidence in the players' minds. It was the belief that they were unbeatable. It was the change in their expectations. Now they knew they could win. To go from defeat to victory all they had to do was to change their mental attitude; to substitute doubt with faith.

Faith power can even help cure fatal diseases, which is why faith healers and mind-body practitioners are becoming more popular. It is well-known that some terminal cancer patients who are given a few months to live suddenly manifest a surprising recovery, which their doctors, unable to explain it, call 'spontaneous remission'. How do these incurable patients manage to recover? In many cases these people claim to have undergone a spiritual experience, or a shift in awareness that changed their belief system and their mental outlook on life. At a certain point, they felt a 'click' or a connection with a higher entity. The so-called placebo effect is another manifestation of faith power. As far back as the First World War wounded soldiers in severe pain were injected with a saline solution when morphine supplies ran out and many of them felt the pain subside as if they had been given morphine. They were actually relieved by the power of mind. As Dr Norman Cousins said, 'Drugs are not always necessary, (but) belief in recovery always is.' The power of mind over matter is a basic fact of life.

Attention and intention release a powerful magnetic power. Whether we want a better job, a new conservatory, a loving relationship or just more money, we only need to constantly contemplate about it, daily. And we must learn to oust any niggling doubts that may come up, because they turn off our power. Attention, however, can be used in several ways: You can think about your goal, talk about it or visualise it. But the quickest way to create your desire is by experiencing it as an existing reality. The greatest attraction force is released through the higher vibrations of enthusiasm and passion. Thoughts and words are all-powerful but the most powerful of all is emotion; what you see for yourself, what you feel. To intensify your power as you visualise, you must bring yourself to feel the excitement of having what you want, as if you already had it now. This is when your creative power is at its peak.

To use this power effectively, we have to change our outlook about what is attainable. Look at the world through rose-coloured glasses. As Francois Guizot remarked, 'The world belongs to the optimists. Pessimists are only spectators.' Optimism is the energy of life. As we practise an optimistic outlook and listen in, we become more receptive and more able to trust the inner whispers, urges and notions that come to guide us. We get more flashes of inspiration and epiphanies which mystics call 'moments of grace'. When this occurs, we must enlist the courage to follow our gut feelings even if they make no sense. Urges, inspirations, premonitions and extra sensory perceptions (ESPs) are the road signs to our goals and to our growth.

Gratefulness boosts your creative power. Counting your blessings helps develop an inner sense of optimism which helps calm down a turbulent mind, improving your connection to the higher dimensions. The more you count your blessings, the more blessings you will have to count. Say 'thank you' more often. Feelings of appreciation and gratitude raise your vibration. They improve your connection with your abstract mind, the part which links the right and left brain, the rational and the intuitive. In full relaxation, you become more perceptive and better able to sense higher forms of notions and insights which are beyond your normal way of thinking. Situations suddenly appear in a different light; solutions to old problems pop up; inspirations, revelations and creative ideas come to light.

We all like to be in control of our lives. When situations get out of hand, however, we tend to lose our self-confidence. We may feel powerless, vulnerable and insecure. Fear of the unknown can set in because we are not completely sure that we are taken care of on a higher level by a loving intelligence that is always leading us to our higher good. Such times are opportunities to grow stronger by taking time to calm down and reflect on the love and wisdom of our higher self. Solutions and clarifications will be revealed if we keep still in a recipient awareness.

Surrendering our need to be in charge and in control every minute is the first step to practising faith in the infinite wisdom of our unconscious mind. Once we set a goal, we must learn to trust our inner guidance to lead us to it. Pre-planning each little detail and constantly watching over everything to make sure nothing goes wrong saps our energy. We must learn to put down this burden and let our inner wisdom be in charge. We must learn to go with the flow of events, whatever they are. We must not interfere or try to force things to happen prematurely. We just need to wait patiently for the messages of our inner guidance to pop up, and act on them. Things may turn out even better than we expected.

One working woman needed to double her income. She started to do spiritual work – that is, to meditate on her goal and visualise her pay rise. The next thing she knew, she got fired. She obviously felt devastated. After the initial shock had subsided, she realised, while meditating on her situation, that she had always had a hidden desire to run a flower shop. By now she was trusting enough to follow her inner urges and in two years' time, she got her desired income in her own flower shop doing a job she enjoyed.

We are not always able to interpret single events that occur in our lives, be they 'fortunate' or 'unfortunate,' because we cannot know the plan of the higher scheme of things. Our higher self may sometimes lead us to our goals via a series of chaotic events. Chaos Theory states that there is order in apparent disorder, that things are not really random, just complex. Most natural processes in this world are chaotic because chaotic systems are driven by a huge number of inputs or factors, the full impact of which cannot be fully considered and is therefore difficult to predict. That is why, in spite of extensive research and state-of-the-art technology, weather forecasts or predictions on the attitude of financial markets are often inaccurate.

Our thoughts create our experiences. Our dreams create our reality. The huge Empire State Building in New York and the tiny computer chip all started with a thought. Martin Luther King 'had a dream' which abolished racial segregation and changed American society forever. The power behind thoughts and dreams, however, is not only infinitely creative, it is also neutral. It will create exactly what we aspire and believe in, both our favourable thoughts and our unfavourable thoughts. As Henry Ford said, 'Whatever you think you can or think you can't, you are right.' That is why we must be careful what we wish for. That is why we must choose only positive thoughts that can benefit us and discard negative ones of fear and doubt that can harm us. We must choose our thoughts wisely.

In *Creative Mind and Success* Ernest Holmes explains,

'We live in mind and it can return to us only what we think into it. No matter what we do, Law will always obtain. If we are thinking of ourselves as poor and needy, then Mind has no choice but to return what we have thought into It. "It is done unto you as you believe."'

Your success does not depend on outer conditions. Deep within your unconscious mind there is an infinite number of ideas that can be converted to cash, regardless of whether the economy is in recession or stocks are in decline. You simply have to sell yourself the idea that adverse conditions which your rational mind interprets as tough breaks are of no consideration to the inner creative power within you, which knows how to overcome any predicament and solve any problem. Look for an opportunity behind any difficulty. All you need to do is to stay focused on your aspiration and not give in when the going gets rough. To develop your creative power you must practise it regularly, with the same motivation and dedication as professional athletes train for competitions.

That which you contemplate becomes the law of your being. Whatever you identify with you become. If you think you have to struggle for anything you want to achieve, you will experience a strenuous life. You will have to work hard for everything. If, on the other hand, you are one of those happy-go-lucky individuals who feel that life is meant to be enjoyed, things will come to you easily and effortlessly. We all have the freedom of choice. You can consciously choose to change your concepts and make life easier by giving your thoughts a new direction. You must never feel helpless or victimised by life. As Benjamin Disraeli said, 'Man is not the creature of circumstances; circumstances are the creatures of man.' The sum total of your life is the sum total of your thoughts. Therefore, think optimistically and change your life.

New thoughts can remake you. The famous American

psychologist and philosopher William James said: 'The greatest discovery of my generation is that human beings can alter their lives by altering their attitudes of mind.' As we go through life we are exposed to new experiences that reshape our concepts and change our reality. We go through thick and thin, through ups and downs. To benefit from our lessons in the school of life, we must learn to draw a distinction, and choose thoughts of faith, love and success that empower us, while rejecting dispirited, unhappy thoughts that weaken us.

To move forward you must enlist the power of decision. Decisions have great magnetic powers. Decisions shape our lives. When you make a firm decision to achieve a goal, come what may, you boost your power of attraction. Your decision sets in motion a series of events. In the words of the great philosopher Goethe, 'Concerning all acts of initiative and creation, there is one elementary truth – that the moment one definitely commits oneself, then Providence moves, too.' When you make a firm decision you become fully committed to its positive outcome; you will disregard your doubts and will not take a 'no' for an answer. With a magnifying glass you can focus the sunlight to light a fire. Likewise, by focusing on your desire you magnify your power in creating the conditions for achievement.

To strengthen a sagging spirit or a weak resolve, pretend to act strong, or, as Alcoholics Anonymous recommend, 'fake it to make it'. Visualise yourself handling various situations with assertiveness and determination. When you feel down, give yourself a pep talk. Use positive affirmations to bolster your confidence in yourself. If, for example, your willpower feels weak, keep repeating to yourself affirmations such as: I am powerful; I am focused; I am a born winner. Insist on being optimistic even when going through a dire situation. Feel the joy and gratification of your accomplished goal which is yet to happen and fantasise

159

giving thanks for it. You are not kidding yourself. You are simply acting out the Buddhist teaching of attracting the positive with positive.

Incorporating the concept of our divine identity into our belief system is the tricky part. Many people can generally accept the concept of a loving providence which is always looking after us; many of us can even reckon that in the higher scheme of things, everything happens for our higher good, including what we label as negative. Yet in the midst of a painful experience, we sometimes forget that great opportunities sometimes come disguised as misfortunes. We often fail to realise that we attract adverse situations for a reason: We may be getting a much-needed lesson, we may be led to pursue a different direction or we may just be paying off an old karmic debt. We are not always aware that the intention of the higher plan for all of us is to have a life of harmony, prosperity and happiness. This is the law of a loving universe. As a result, many of us do not claim our inborn right to prosper and are satisfied with shallow achievements. So many of us do not feel worthy of excellence. We fear that asking for 'too much' may be outrageous.

It can take years of consistent spiritual work to drive these truths deep into our unconscious mind, the seat of our power which determines the way we react to challenging situations. To drive home these tenets I personally found it helpful to repeat frequently the following affirmation which, with time, helped me change my mental attitude and consequently upgrade my situation: 'I now claim my right to have unlimited goodness in my life.'

For many years I did not recognise my own divinity. I could only conceive of myself as having limited human abilities, able to accomplish only average achievements that could be accepted by my limited intellect. I did not realise that the power within is limitless. I did not believe in thought power. But one day I heard the epigram, 'God gives you according to your acceptance of the infinite.' In a flash I realised that this was the missing link. It suddenly became clear that my God-given power, which is limitless, is limited only by my own ability to allow it into my life.

Following a car crash, a sweet old granny was shocked to see her grandson trapped under a vehicle. She immediately leapt to the rear of the car and with a superhuman effort managed to raise it enough to release the toddler. What made her astounding feat seem even more incredible was the fact that this little old lady always led a sedentary lifestyle and never exercised. When she was later asked by the press about her feelings following the event, she said that she was sad. When the reporter asked why, she answered: 'Discovering what my potential energy could do, I feel very sad realising how I wasted my life selling myself short.'

Energy can be manifested in various forms, from the unseen spiritual energy to the dense energy of solid matter. For many centuries, Eastern mystics claimed that our physical world is not made up of separate entities, but is actually one big spiritual oneness. Modern quantum physics was finally able to prove that the atom, the so-called basic unit of matter, is not a solid particle. It is composed of sub-atomic particles which are, at their core, specific vibrations of energy. Different atoms of different elements are simply different vibrations in a unified field of energy, which has a potential of infinite creativity.

When we realise that matter is energy, it is easier to conceive that our thoughts, words, feelings, intentions and desires are actually fluctuations of the same kind of energy which is the basic raw material of the universe. Quantum physics tells us that light can be either a particle or a wave, depending on what we expect it to be. Similarly, we can make a goal happen by merely expecting it. To create better and higher experiences in our lives, we simply need to raise the level of our expectations. Once we believe that the power of expectation can make everything possible, we can relax and allow this power to initiate a complex chain of events which will unfold at its own pace, to bring about our desire easily and effortlessly through the law of attraction.

'. . . The action of thought power is not limited to a circumscribed individuality. What the individual does is to give direction to something which is unlimited, to call into action a force infinitely greater than his own, which because it is in itself impersonal though intelligent, will receive the impress of his personality, and can therefore make its influence felt far beyond the limits which bound the individual's objective perception of the circumstances with which he has to deal.' Thomas Troward, Edinburgh lectures.

Before taking action, however, make sure your goal is for your higher good and in compliance with your belief system. It is useless to continue if you have the slightest doubt. The light of your optimism cannot pierce the fog of your doubt. You have to feel in your heart of hearts that you were meant to have your goal and are fully entitled to it. Keep replaying in your mind the gratifying scenario of having it. Then step back and allow your magic to work for you. You must not interfere with its actions, but let your goal come naturally, rather than forcibly pursuing it. Most of all have patience. Trust that your request has been heard and that a power beyond your understanding is working to bring about its creation. Patience calms restlessness. By being patient you are demonstrating your faith and willingness to go at a pace set by your inner power, not at the hasty pace of your intellect. When life goes at one pace and you at another, you are ripping yourself apart. My old gym trainer used to say to me: 'If things go your way, there is no need to rush; and if they don't, why are you rushing?'

Many people are sceptical about their creative abilities.

They do not believe in the limitlessness of their creative power because some things they once wished for did not happen. There are several reasons why some desires are not met. In many cases people fail to achieve because although they pay lip service to their goal, deep down they have niggling doubts about it. It becomes a kind of wishful thinking. In hindsight they will comment that 'anyway, it was too good to be true'. In such cases, the creative power was neutralised because its greatest booster, the faith that can 'move mountains', was not there to back it up. Wishful thinking is a faithless desire. It is tantamount to negative thinking because at a certain deep level, a contemplation of failure produces an energy that opposes creation. A cart pulled by two horses in two different directions can hardly move forward. Likewise, you must have the combined driving forces of mind and heart to move on. To become an achiever, you must say what you mean and mean what you say.

Some requests for material things may be denied by the soul because they will not be for your higher good. You may wish, for example, for a lot of money, but you may not be ready to handle it, or if you had it, it could have harmed you. In such cases, your higher self, which always leads you to your higher good, will instead send you lessons to prepare for it.

When a specific request for money is put on hold, it may be easier to ask for the basic essence of your request. What actually do you expect to do with more money? Could you afford a new car? Would you be able to improve your home, go on a long-yearned-for holiday or give your children a better education? Visualise yourself enjoying these activities rather than the money needed for them, and you can create them quicker in unexpected, alternative ways, not necessarily by having more money.

Obviously, it is important to ask wisely rather than waste

time pursuing unworthy or unsuitable requests that may be denied. Therefore, before deciding on a goal, always confer with yourself. Take time to reflect in what way this goal can serve your higher purpose. Think carefully if it will be for your higher good. Make sure that it will increase your joy, your love and your positive contribution to the welfare of others.

Our higher self needs time to create our goals. There may be challenges on the way, tangles in the road, obstacles to overcome or mountains to climb. Whatever happens, never let your faith falter. Never let your doubts erode your resolve. Keep your thoughts focused on the final goal. The adversities which cross our path are there not to deter us, but to teach us tolerance and perseverance.

We each express our self-love by pursuing our dreams. So follow your dreams, however incredible they may seem. Remember the inspiring words of the late Christopher Reeve: 'At first, dreams seem impossible, then improbable and eventually inevitable.'

Some goals take longer than others to achieve. Some can take days while others can take years. During the time gap between desiring and achieving, we have to remain committed. Patience is an attribute of our inner faith. Patience gives us staying power. Creative power must always be accompanied by patience and persistence. Many underachievers are quitters. They quit prematurely and thus fail to achieve. Let us all reiterate the words of Duke Ellington: 'Life has two rules: Number one, never quit. Number two, always remember rule number one.'

11

Recognising Life's Purpose

Life is a spiritual quest for self-discovery. It has been given to us as a gift by a loving universe to grow to higher levels of happiness by learning valuable lessons in the art of human existence. We came here because our soul has decided that it is time to incarnate in order to heal our spirit and evolve our virtues. As Seneca said, 'Seek the health of your soul. Where does it lie? In not finding your pleasures in deception.' We are here to learn to disown the ego's fearful deceptions and realise that in our essence, we are pure love and bliss. In our essence, we are each an incarnated divinity.

Just as children inherit their parents' characteristics, similarities and genes, so do we spiritually inherit from our creator's divine qualities such as love, power, creativity and compassion. God's spiritual DNA is encoded in each soul. But just as any inborn talent can only be developed by practising it, so can we develop the divine qualities of our higher nature only by focusing our attention on them. And as we keep dwelling on them, we develop an ever-increasing awareness of our divine potential. We evolve by learning to give and receive love freely. We grow to overcome the fear of the ego by practising faith attitudes in the benevolence of life which is always there for us, never against us. Rumi, the thirteenth-century Sufi mystic, wrote, 'Kill the cow of your ego as quickly as you can, so that your inner spirit can come to life and attain true awareness.' We grow to higher awareness by using faith to hack away fear. We grow more powerful by trusting life to sustain us and by coming to realise that everything happens for a higher reason.

The fourteenth-century Kabbalist Moses De Leon wrote in his *Book of Wise Soul*: 'To enter the inner sanctum one must know his soul which is modelled on the soul of his creator.' We were created 'in the image and likeliness of God', and our souls are a reflection of the divine. We are here to discover our divine identity and manifest our inner potential. When we realise that we are each part of the divine spirit, it becomes easier to develop a feeling of inner identity with higher states of love, power and compassion.

We need to be willing to transcend our shortcomings and evolve, because this is really what we are here for. Our growth is our own contribution to making the world a better place. As Leo Tolstoy said, 'Everyone thinks of changing the world but no one thinks of changing himself.' We are here to relearn that as individualised parts of God, we are actually God's co-creators. We must never underestimate ourselves. What we each do affects the whole planet. With a stronger sense of inner connectedness it is easier to trust the universe and keep going with the flow in the face of the uncertainties that are part and parcel of life.

We grow spiritually by being of service to others. Trying to help other people less fortunate than ourselves is the highest moral right and the purpose of our existence. We each have a specific contribution to make to an important cause in this world. From street sweepers and beggars to Nobel laureates and financial tycoons, we all have a mission to accomplish, our soul's calling. It is just that we often get so caught up in the humdrum of daily life, that we forget it. Never question the importance of your existence. Although you may not be aware of it, you are here according to a higher plan, to serve a purpose, to make a difference. And

166

as you love yourself and evolve, you increasingly realise your unique importance.

We are all sustained and loved by a higher form of intelligence which wants all of us to be happy and fulfilled in everything we do. We can create any reality we choose to believe in, be it pleasant or unpleasant, just by using the law of attraction. If we choose to believe in a friendly world, we will eventually create this reality for ourselves and will experience an amicable planet. But this will be *our* reality, not necessarily that of others.

For many years I used to think that there is only one reality, the one I noticed and experienced around me. That was before I knew that each person lives in a different reality which is a reflection of their concepts and beliefs. One man's reason is another man's folly. Someone's treasures are another person's trifles. A million dollars can seem a huge fortune to one but peanuts to a billionaire. For the six billion people in this world there are six billion different realities! We cannot criticise the action of other people because we each live in a different psyche. That is why the ancient Jewish mystics coined the phrase, 'Do not judge your friend until you stand in his place.'

We have incarnated into this world to rise to higher levels of awareness in order to realise our divine identity. We are here to purify our thinking and become more virtuous. Working, having relationships, raising a family and all our mundane activities is what we do to sustain life and provide learning opportunities for growth. The more we perceive anything we do and anything that happens to us with spiritual orientation, the more we can interpret the inner meaning of events. As we grow, we come to realise that the spiritual self is much more powerful than the physical self. And as we do so, we learn to live more in the spiritual and less in the physical.

We are not human beings having a spiritual experience;

we are spiritual beings having a human experience. Our normal state of being is spiritual. We are souls. Being physical is only a transient phase in our eternal existence. The lifetime we were given on this planet is actually an education term. The whole world is our campus. Our soul sent us here to grow. Growth involves going through uncomfortable experiences, releasing hurts and moving ahead. Growth involves allowing life to teach us and heal us. And as we send love to our lower emotions, we heal them. We upgrade them into elevated virtues of higher vibrations.

To expand life and make it more meaningful, we do not have to retreat into a cave, become a recluse and meditate all day long, because it is the daily challenges of our relationships that teach us unconditional love. We have to live in the world of our calling and make use of our inborn creativity; to conceive and accomplish goals that will make our life happier and more fulfilled; to make a difference; to let our talents and skills contribute to the welfare of humanity.

Living life to the full and being involved is part of our purpose. Making your daily life work, attending to your relationships and career, paying your bills, taking care of yourself and becoming self-sufficient are all as important as meditation. Daily chores like washing dishes, doing the laundry, shopping or driving to work can all become opportunities for growth if you view them from a higher perspective. Every person we meet and every event we encounter can help accelerate our growth by providing insights and morals, if only we would calm down and pause to reflect on their inner meanings. Everyone and everything around us are our teachers; they all provide insights which can lead us to understand things from a higher perspective.

One of the most important decisions you could ever make is to believe in yourself and trust the universe. Believe in yourself as a focus of divinity and trust in the universe as a caring foster parent. Do not waver even if circumstances around you do not support your expectations. Do not be tempted to reconsider your commitment even during a dire situation. When a plan crashes or a venture fails, we may temporarily become frustrated, depressed, vulnerable or insecure. These experiences, as difficult as they are, offer an opportunity to boost strength of character and moral fibre. When things fall apart do not panic. Do not be tempted to sit on the pity pot and cry, 'Why me?' Try instead to relax. Sit down and calmly reflect on your situation from a higher level. Remember that every cloud has a silver lining. Ask your higher self what this experience is trying to tell you; what the moral of the story is. When we feel stretched to the limit, we are given a golden chance to practise self-love and reject self-torture. We are given a chance to practise faith in the power that sustains us. Actually, we attract painful experiences for these very reasons.

All six billion of us on this planet are musicians in a divine symphony orchestra, of which God is the conductor. Our concert is pre-composed and we each play a different instrument and a different tone. If we follow the conductor's instructions, harmonious music will sound. If, however, we ignore the conductor's lead and play our part as we see fit, we create disharmony with the rest of the orchestra. We spoil a divine music. The conductor leads us to play a tune of divine harmony and love, while we often choose to play the acrimonious tunes of our fearful ego. We forget that the universe operates according to a higher harmonious order. As Albert Einstein said, 'The more I study the universe the more I believe in a higher power.'

Life is constantly providing growth lessons through various occurrences and opportunities, successes and failures, joys and sorrows. We are all so impacted by major events that we forget that every little thing, too, has an inner meaning; every tiny event has a message. According to the ancient Jewish mystics, 'No person moves his finger down here unless it is ordained up there.' The slightest thing in life happens for a reason. Most of us miss the subtle significance of these mini-lessons because we are not aware of their importance. To hear the messages we need to set aside time to be on our own, and quietly reflect on things. We need to listen with a peaceful mind in order to hear the call of grace.

All too often we tend to ignore our inner premonitions. My friend recently brought a glass of water to the bathroom when she got a strange persistent feeling that the glass was about to break. She dismissed this feeling, thinking to herself, 'Come on, I never break anything.' A couple of minutes later, as she was reaching for a brush, her hand tipped the glass, which fell down and smashed.

Many people often feel a shift in consciousness following a major physical or emotional crisis. When daunting situations like fatal diseases, life-threatening accidents, and drug or alcohol addictions are suddenly followed by an inexplicable cure or a miraculous rescue, people feel that a higher power, whether they call it God, Fate or Providence, has intervened to snatch them from the throes of death. They undergo a spiritual experience. Something inside clicks. They suddenly feel different from within. They start seeing things in a different light. The petty things that previously used to bother them become meaningless. They become more discerning. They start appreciating the real values of life. A spiritual experience is a great gift. It is a quantum leap to a higher level of awareness. It is really what we are here for.

Sometimes you may feel that it is all too much. Life's troubles have become too stressful for comfort, things have gone too far, lessons have become too hard. When you feel fed up with what life is throwing at you and you want to bail out, you may wish to say, 'Stop the world, I want to get off,' but you can't. You are here for the duration. Like a person who finds himself compelled to play a game of poker but is dealt a deck of cards which he does not like, you cannot leave. You must play your hand to the best of your ability. If life gives you a lemon, make it into a lemonade.

When overwhelmed with what may seem to be catastrophic or insurmountable problems, it is very tempting for some people to contemplate suicide and put an end to it all. They do not realise that they are intervening with the divine plan of the soul. They are cutting short their pre-planned evolution course in this lifetime and will have to come back and start again from the point where they left off. It is best to nip suicidal tendencies in the bud. In the long run, no one can play truant in the school of life.

When going through an adverse phase in which nothing seems to make sense any more, it is easy to feel a victim of fate and indulge in self-pity. Instead, change your thoughts. Visualise life from a higher perspective. We are all temporary inhabitants on a ball spinning in space. Billions come to visit. None stay. All return sooner or later to other worlds. And while they are here, what are they here for? They come for the chaos, the uncertainty and the irrational, not for the logic or the ability to explain everything. Life is a mystery. Life is full of surprises. Sometimes, for life to make sense, we should stop looking for sense and accept uncertainty because uncertainty is often a gateway to opportunity. The easier way to go is to develop a blind faith in the uncertainties of life: to believe that no matter what happens, life works perfectly; to believe that in the higher scheme of things everything happens for our higher good; to believe that what we are going through is exactly what we need in order to grow and evolve to our full potential as human beings in a perfect universe.

As rational human beings we seek rhyme and reason in everything. However, as mystics have been saying all along, the world consists of the known, the unknown and the unknowable. We can strive to understand the unknown but can never reach the unknowable. We all know the law of gravity, but do we know why it works? Why should two masses attract each other in the first place? For all our sophistication we do not even understand how come we stay put on this earth. As Thomas Edison said, 'We don't even begin to understand one per cent about ninety nine per cent of everything.' Life will always be greater than our ability to comprehend it.

Try not to get too involved in life. Whatever happens, distance yourself a bit from reality. And as you rise to a higher vantage point, you can get glimpses of the bigger picture. You are better able to read the map. As Emily Dickinson wrote, 'The soul should always stand ajar, ready to welcome the ecstatic experience.' Do not try so hard to intervene and manipulate. Instead, let life unfold and just contemplate about the inner meaning of events that come up. There is a wealth of knowledge to be gained by backing off a little, by just being.

Seen from a higher perspective, life is a miraculous experience. In spite of what 'realistic' cynics say, our lives are known to contain inexplicable spontaneous phenomena such as synchronicities, serendipities or unexpected flukes and windfalls. Miracles, however, come in many forms, some more ostentatious and some more subtle. Incredibly, they can sometimes appear as a painful experience or a crisis situation which later, in hindsight, is recognised as a 'blessing in disguise'. *The hardest part of a miracle is to interpret it as a blessing when it comes in such inauspicious forms as a failure, a setback, an accident or a fatal disease.*

Many people feel that life events are a mixture of fate and luck, but only few sense that their life follows a preordained script. To highly evolved individuals it is obvious that much like a movie screenplay, there is a script for every life. The traditional view, to which Plato subscribed, is that you choose the story of your life before birth and are bound to follow it. Your script determines where and when you are born, who your parents are and what lessons are planned for you during this lifetime. Thereafter, you are free to go your own way, subject to the script. You may think you can choose to get away and change course arbitrarily, but whatever you do, it is all in the script.

The dilemma between destiny and free will has been baffling philosophers since ancient times. If everything is predestined, what role does free will play? Can our spontaneous choices interfere with our fate? Imagine a ship on course to a port of call. If the captain makes a navigational error, it will take the ship longer to get to its destination. In this lifetime, we are each assigned a unique calling. We are each called to serve humanity in our own distinct way while learning specific virtues such as love, patience and generosity, which we have to pursue as our destination. When we make a choice which is not compatible with our assigned lesson or calling, it will simply take us longer to reach our goals. Ultimately, our freedom of choice rests with our ability to accelerate or slow down our evolution.

Our souls are constantly striving towards greater growth, expansion, changes and challenges. This may cause inner conflicts. Some parts of our personalities understand the need for growth and change, while other parts resist the change and prefer to cling to the familiar 'devil we know'. At the end of the day, every painful crisis on our path is a healing experience. As hard as some phases in life can be, they are actually opportunities to exercise a stronger faith in the higher power that loves us and sustains us. And the more we lift our faith, the more we overcome our fears. Faith lift is much more important than a face lift.

Occasionally, the path of growth involves going through a period of a major life-transforming crisis. It may feel as if you lost your foothold, or that you are going through a void of emptiness where nothing is familiar. It is a period of time between projects or between changing lifestyles. Some common examples are when you lose a job and wonder what to do next, when you end a relationship or lose a loved one and find yourself alone, when you are forced to retire, or when you need to relocate and find a new home.

Going through a void is an intense emotional experience. I know, because I have been there. You feel lost and insecure. You are in a limbo. You become very sensitive over different issues. You find yourself questioning everything. Your minds gets flooded with questions such as, 'Where am I going from here?' 'What has become of me?' 'How can I survive?' 'What is the purpose of all this?' It is a period of soul searching. You may feel a greater need for sleep or feel less energetic. You may become less sociable. You may prefer to be on your own and less inclined for physical intimacy with another. You need time to develop the connection to your higher self. The more time you spend on your own, the more you get in touch with your feelings and emotions, the better you get to know yourself and understand what's right for you.

As uncomfortable and terrifying as it may feel, the void is a great spiritual gift. It is a period of accelerated growth. You are letting go of a certain level of personality which does not fit you anymore and taking a quantum leap to a higher level of awareness of love and confidence. And although nothing seems to be happening externally, much is happening internally. The uncertainty of this experience offers new choices. It opens up a new range of options, previously unimaginable. It gives you an opportunity to go for cherished goals and create a much better future. So in the middle of all the gloom, try to keep optimistic. Although you may not have the foggiest clue how things will turn out, tell yourself that in one way or another, everything is happening for your higher good. Then, as life gets back

174

again on an even keel and things start to make more sense, you will know that you have left the void. You will emerge a changed person. You will have gained a different view of life. You will see things from a higher perspective. You will feel that you have evolved.

Resisting painful experiences causes needless suffering. By resisting a painful experience we refuse our life-script and miss an important part of our spiritual education. Pain is part of life. Pain is a teacher and a healer. It urges us to realise that everything happens for our higher good and that sometimes, wrong things happen for the right reason. Painful times lead us to higher understandings. That is why we create them. Rather than resisting pain, relax and listen in. Pain can help open you up to new revelations and lead you to correct your thinking if you lost your orientation. In painful times you are closest to your soul, and therefore, more open to receive higher knowledge about the deeper meaning of love as your ultimate goal. You may get a sharper distinction about what's important versus what's trivial. So let pain purge your personality and refine your ego. As philosopher Simone Weil said, 'The great strength of Christianity is that it proposes not a remedy for suffering, but a use for it.'

While pain is inevitable, suffering is optional. Emotional suffering depends on the way we interpret our situation and react to it. If we take things too personally – that is, if we keep playing the victim in our mind over and over, become resentful and think that our pain is pointless or unfair – we increase suffering. If, on the other hand, we realise that that our pain has a purpose and that in some inconceivable way it is meant to assist our growth and lead us to a higher level of fulfilment, suffering is greatly reduced. Victor Frankl, the Viennese psychiatrist who survived the atrocities of Auschwitz in World War II, said, 'Man is ready to shoulder any suffering as soon and as long as he can see meaning to it.'

We have to cultivate the concept that painful or joyful, every event we attract to our life has a meaning. Everything that happens is designed to help us grow and evolve. Setbacks must not be feared because setbacks often turn out to become stepping-stones to breakthroughs.

We have been given the mirror effect to help us recognise and identify the ailing parts of our spirit which need healing. Just as we need a mirror to see our eyes which are a reflection of our souls, we similarly need a mirror to reflect back to us our erroneous thoughts and concepts. Our reality is this mirror. For better or for worse, our reality reflects back to us our mental attitudes. A fulfilling situation reflects a positive idea, just as a distressing situation reflects back an erroneous thought. Poverty reflects concepts of scarcity just as popularity reflects a loving, non-judgemental character. As we intensify our self-love, increase our self-confidence and boost our optimism, more fortuitous events will accordingly be reflected in our reality.

When things seem to be going against us, they are only reflecting back to us obstructions in our power flow. They highlight faulty parts in our belief system that need to be upgraded. Our problems will keep on repeating themselves until we recognise the lower thinking patterns that are holding us down, which need to be discarded and substituted with higher ones. If you keep attracting abusive people, they are simply reflecting back to you your own self-abuse; if people are lying to you, you are in certain ways lying to yourself; if people walk all over you, you feel unworthy because you have forgotten your divine identity. When we finally get the message and upgrade a lower thought to a higher level, the problem stops; it has served its purpose. Evolving various aspects of self-love is what spiritual growth is all about.

It has been said that love makes the world go round. This is not just a nice lyric. It is not a fantasy, nor an illusion nor a metaphor, but the absolute truth. Love is the energy of life. Love is the power that sustains the universe. Hate is a destructive energy that destroys it. Love is light, hate is darkness. Love makes the wheat grow and the birds sing. Hate makes war and disease. If only more people could realise how deep this principle is, they would start to increase their own self-love, in order to increase their ability to spread love and light, which is our life's purpose.

Love refines our physical appearance. It softens our face lines. One of the perks of spiritual growth is enhanced physical attraction. As you raise your awareness and become more loving and happy, your features release more charm and loveliness. You become more attractive. The light that shines in your aura becomes more brilliant. Love adds beauty to everything. Love transforms the plain to the pretty. Remember occasions when you were surprised to see dramatic changes for the better in the appearance of people you have not met for years? They suddenly looked younger or prettier that you remembered them. They seemed as if they were enlightened. You know that these people have grown.

However, just as some people use the lessons of life experiences to upgrade their concepts and grow to higher states of consciousness, others choose to defy their lessons and go against the grain. Losing faith in life and disowning their inner connection to a loving universe, they start visualising any adversity as 'punishment' by an unfair fate. Fear and insecurity grow. Love and confidence decline. Bitterness takes over. They do not realise that any setback is designed as a lesson for growth by a higher loving power. Gradually they become cynical and 'realistic' about life. This can easily be noticed in university reunions, when twenty or thirty years after graduation, the beauty of some students from school days has faded, whereas some formerly plain students have become gorgeous ladies or charming gentlemen. They simply have the beauty of their rich spiritual evolution written on their faces.

In our growth path, self-love is a panacea, a cure-all energy. It can help heal physical and mental conditions alike because it is a multi-purpose, all-creative energy. It is the source of anything good. When you cultivate self-love, you commit to validate, support and respect yourself, not in some future time, but right now. You commit to honour your needs; you acknowledge your uniqueness regardless of what other people think; you assert yourself with compassion; you realise that you are all-powerful because you are one with the power that created you. Therefore, you will not allow anyone to control you in any way, nor will you try to control others, as you appreciate their own divinity. You know that you are lovable and expect people to love you as you are. You will communicate from your heart, the seat of unconditional love, and will consequently treat yourself and others gently and compassionately.

In our culture, money counts. Our society judges people's success by the size of their bank account, by how much they are 'worth'. Indeed, most people believe that financial success is a primary aspiration. The more money you amass, the more admiration you command. The ultimate purpose of life, however, is not to idolise money, but to aspire to enrich your inner world and realise that you are being taken care of by a loving universe. Financial prosperity is eventually a by-product of a prosperous state of mind.

Having worshipped the idol of money for many years, there are people who become materialistically very successful. Some even become wealthy. However, once a certain financial level is achieved, many start to feel as if something is missing. They are not comfortable at a soul level. There is a feeling of emptiness from within. All their riches do not make them satisfied, fulfilled and secure as they once thought. Money suddenly appears as a false deity. They become disillusioned, and this prompts them to start looking for the real purpose of life, to seek an inner connection and aspire to grow.

I like to compare our allotted lifetime to military service. When we are drafted, we are sent to an induction base where we are supplied with all the equipment we need. We then start basic training. Subsequently, there are many different vocational courses available, and each soldier is assigned to a suitable one before being posted to his or her unit. Throughout the service, all are expected to do their duty to the best of their ability. The better they do, the higher they get promoted. Many do not bother much and remain privates. Others with more motivation and capability rise up to become NCOs or officers. Through continuous training and battle experience, enlisted soldiers get opportunities to distinguish themselves and rise to higher proficiency levels. However, when their time is up, each one returns his or her gear and is discharged. They only take with them non-tangible assets such as skills, expertise and assertiveness, which are usually symbolised by the rank they managed to acquire during their service.

It is similar in life. We arrive here as babies with nothing and are immediately supplied with all we need. We spend our growing years in schools which are our basic training. When we graduate as adults, life assigns us to different courses in varying degrees of hardship in accordance with our individual growth needs, to help us get stronger and evolve to a higher level or 'rank'. No two people get exactly the same life script because each person needs different growth lessons and sometimes even to pay karmic debts from previous lifetimes. Each life is unique. That is why different people handle life's trials differently. And as in the army, some are willing to heed the call of grace while others do not bother. Which is why some people seem as if they are doomed to struggle throughout their life, constantly repeating their mistakes, while other learn and grow. When our time is up, we leave behind all the material things that we have acquired such as money, assets and relationships, and return to the source. The only thing we take with us to the other side is the karma we earned and the higher consciousness, the 'rank' we managed to achieve. In this world we actually do not own anything. Everything we have is on loan from the universe to be used only while we are here.

In the army, any soldier has the potential to become a high-ranking officer. Napoleon said that every private has the baton of a field-marshal in his kitbag. Not many, however, have the motivation or the leadership capability. Very few are motivated enough to put up with all the hard training required to move up. Even many capable soldiers who could easily become officers simply do not want the extra responsibility that comes with a higher rank. They prefer to do only the minimum duties required and kill time until discharge.

In civilian life, as in the army, we all have the potential to rise to higher 'ranks' of awareness. All of us who wake up to join the growth path become active recruits in an evolutionary army. Our job in this army is to evolve our souls by healing them, and help others to heal theirs. To do a good job we need to develop a loving consciousness by increasing self-love. Not everyone joins this evolution campaign. Many people do not wake up to heed the call of grace. They are too lazy to devote the time and effort. As Jesus said, 'Many are called but few are chosen.'

Being of service to others accelerates our growth. As we empower other people and show them the way to claim their own power, we are also empowering ourselves. When we advise other people how to become more self-confident, we create an opportunity for all of us to grow. When we devote ourselves to the higher good of others, we simultaneously enhance our own good. Our aura becomes more radiant. We become more magnetic to good things. We attract better opportunities, increased prosperity and more loving people into our lives. Serving the higher good of others makes us happier and more fulfilled.

Practising unity with the universe intensifies our sense of connectedness. It is so normal to perceive cars, houses, trees, dolphins and other people as separate entities, that most of us have a problem realising the oneness of reality. All along history, however, Buddhists and Hindu mystics have been professing that our common perception of the world as containing separate entities is an illusion, or 'Maya', because everything is simply a different manifestation of the same all-creative energy. We are one with everything. To realise oneness, however, we have to forego our ego because it is impossible to feel universal unity through the limiting boundaries of the ego which perpetuates separateness. We evolve by learning to loosen the hold of the ego and becoming somewhat like little tots who feel one with everything around them during the first months of their lives, because their ego has not yet developed. As adults, though, we need to reconcile our individuality with our oneness. When you merge with the higher consciousness of oneness, you do not renounce your individuality; you accentuate it as a part of the bigger unity. You actually grow stronger.

A few years ago, at the Seattle Special Olympics for the physically or mentally disabled, nine runners stood ready at the starting line for the hundred yard dash. At the gunshot, they all started to run, not in such a great sprint but nevertheless with a great desire to win. One little boy stumbled on the track, tumbled over and began to cry. The other runners slowed down and looked over their shoulders. Then they all turned back to the boy. One girl with Down's Syndrome bent and kissed the hurting boy, saying, 'This will make it better.' Then all the contestants joined hands and together walked to the finish line. Everybody in the stadium stood up. The ecstatic cheering went on for several minutes. Everyone was touched. Why? Because these kids demonstrated human oneness at its best. They showed that we all win when one of us wins.

Intrigued by such things as telepathy, telekinesis and ESP, Professor Robert Jahn of Princeton University began researching paranormal phenomena during the late 1970s by using a Random Event Generator which produces even amounts of ones and zeros. He then hauled passers-by in from the street and asked them to concentrate their minds on his numeral generator. He was in fact asking them to mentally flip more ones than zeros. As preposterous as this idea may sound, the results were astounding. Again and again, ordinary people could influence the machine with their thoughts to produce uneven amounts of 'heads' and 'tails', as was recorded on a graph.

In a later study called the Global Consciousness Project, Dr Roger Nelson extended this research by placing 40 Random Event Generators all over the world and connecting them to his laboratory in Princeton. These ran together consistently, producing a flat graph on his computer. But one day, on 6 September 1997, something extraordinary happened. The graph shot upwards, recording a sudden shift in number sequences as the machines around the world started reporting huge deviations from the norm. That day was when one billion people around the world watched the funeral procession of Diana, Princess of Wales. The global outburst of emotion was for the first time detected and measured. But the greatest enigmatic finding was yet to come on 11 September 2001, when the generators (or 'eggs') registered a huge shift four hours *before* the attack on the Twin Towers in New York. These studies have demonstrated not only the interconnection of human consciousness, but also the existence of collective unconsciousness, our inherent infinite wisdom, which is able even to predict future events. It revealed the protective presence of grace within us.

Grace is a loving energy that works in mysterious ways to sustain our life and nurture our growth. Grace is incomprehensible and miraculous. It can be manifested internally, through urges, feelings and premonitions of the unconscious mind, or externally, through lucky coincidences and fortuitous events. Miracles are not just a biblical myth; they are a common daily phenomenon. To notice the miracles of grace more often, we must simply pay more attention to daily events. We all hear from time to time how a person walked unscathed out of a totally crushed car, or how against all odds, a few people survived a plane crash. But daily miracles are more subtle. When a problem is troubling you and suddenly, out of the blue, you meet someone who provides you with the solution, this is your miracle. If you contemplate on such unpredictable flukes, you will become increasingly aware that your life is indeed magical.

Spiritual growth itself is a miracle. In our world, everything ages and disintegrates. Given time, everything is reduced from neat to messy, from a higher order to a lower order. So does our body and so should our consciousness. This is what the second Law of Thermodynamics tells us. Spiritual evolution, however, is an exception to this natural law. By aspiring to evolve, we defy the law of nature and go against the grain. As we grow, we actually reverse the ageing process of our spirit. Instead of deteriorating into a lower nature we evolve into a higher awareness. And as we grow spiritually, we rise into a higher level of existence.

Every quantum leap to a higher level of consciousness makes the next stage easier. We may spend years laying a foundation and then one day, out of the blue, we feel a click, a shift in perception, a leap in awareness. From then on our lives are no longer the same. We think and feel differently. The way we relate to the world has changed. With time, the growth path itself becomes quicker. As we no longer resist as we used to, it becomes easier to adopt new concepts of higher awareness on our path to enlightenment.

Enlightenment, however, is not a final destination that we reach and can then rest on our laurels. It is a never-ending story. It is an ongoing process, for no matter how high we get, there are always higher levels to reach. The more enlightened we become, the greater our ability to have clarity, harmony and love in anything we do. Our greatest quest in life is self knowledge. As the Tao Te Ching says: 'It is wisdom to know others; It is enlightenment to know one's self.'

Grace is the divine expression of God's love for us. Counting the blessings of grace in our lives can enhance our inner connectedness to the higher love that enfolds us. It is a way to achieve the love, the power and the faith that we need in order to have a meaningful life. It is the way to our divine purpose.

The famous hymn by John Newton is a wonderful illustration of our relationship to grace:

> Amazing grace! How sweet the sound
> That saved a wretch like me!
> I once was lost but now I am found,
> Was blind but now I see.
>
> 'Twas grace that taught my heart to fear,
> And grace my fears relieved;
> How precious did that grace appear
> The hour I first believed.

Through many dangers, toils and snares,
I have already come;
'Tis grace hath brought me safe thus far,
And grace will lead me home.

And when we've been here ten thousand years,
Bright shining as the sun,
We'll have no less days to sing God's praise
Than when we first begun.

12

Welcoming Change

Nothing stands still. Life is a dynamic experience and change is a natural part of it. From germs and flowers to coastlines and galaxies, everything is constantly adapting to changing conditions by mutating, transforming and recreating. This is how life develops and evolves. Likewise, this is how we, as human beings, grow to higher levels of awareness and happiness. This is how we rise to our higher good. Yet many people are wary of change. They are reluctant to open up to the new, preferring to stay with the familiar reality, however unsatisfactory.

Our very existence means changing and evolving. It is important to realise that mankind could not have survived, let alone developed, without constant change. And in order to keep on living and evolving we are from time to time required to face a new situation, dare a new challenge or adapt to new circumstances. The problem is that altering a tried-and-tested lifestyle usually involves a risk which often feels daunting or unsafe. But trying to live without taking risks is against the very nature of life. It is counterproductive. Life is an ongoing adventure and unpredictable changes are part of our evolution. It is by daring to take on life's challenges that we move forwards and upwards. As the famous motto coined by Colonel David Sterling when he founded the British S.A.S. goes, 'Who dares wins.'

Change opens the way for progress. Welcoming new

ideas, new situations and new people into our life increases our capacity to have more: More happiness, more fulfilment, more abundance and more love. The reason many people will not let go of the past and embrace the new is their lack of faith in the all-sustaining power of life which has always, and will always, lead us to our higher good.

Fear of the future prevents many people from contemplating any change. As a result, they won't dare to upset the apple cart. They are not ready to consider that change is an opportunity for something better. In fact, life itself is a series of unpredictable changes. Get married, and your spouse may divorce you or die, leaving you with a deep pain; have children, and they can become a disappointment; start a business, and it may crash and make you bankrupt. But avoiding taking chances is like avoiding life itself. It is a contracting and diminishing of the self to the point of non-existence.

Each time we do something new we gain experience, whether we succeed or not. Each attempt is a step forward on the road towards a higher level of success. In this sense, success is a way of life, not necessarily an immediate goal. Thomas Alva Edison, the American genius of technology who held patents for scores of inventions, conducted thousands of experiments in order to create the first light bulb. Was he discouraged after each failed experiment? Did he bemoan his luck? Was he willing to give up? Of course not! He would not let failures stop him. From the knowledge he gained from each failed attempt he went on to the next one. When quizzed by a reporter after one of his unsuccessful trials, he said, 'We have just discovered another way how the incandescent lamp won't work.' Experience is what enables future success. Having gone through two divorces or having failed in three businesses should not stop you from trying again and again and ultimately becoming successful.

Constant upgrading of attitudes of mind is what spiritual growth is all about. Life keeps steering us towards higher levels of love and awareness by creating perfectly designed events which urge us to discard old views, adopt new concepts and embrace higher thought patterns. Our ability to open up to these changes and flow with them determines how fast we grow.

The fear of change is the fearful voice of an unreal, fictitious emotion which tries to halt our evolution. It is the voice of the ego. It is perfectly normal to have niggling concerns of vulnerability before allowing new people or new situations into our lives. Do not feel, however, that you must conquer your anxiety before you go out and make things happen. The tension and stress that accompany such situations can instead be regarded as an uplifting of your spiritual vibration into a higher frequency. They are a build up of electromagnetic energy which is preparing you for the change. When you finally come to believe that *everything* happens for your higher good, it is easier to accept changing circumstances and go along with them.

A time of change is an opportunity to develop faith in yourself, faith in other people and faith in life. It is a chance to break free from any attachments you may have to things and situations that have exceeded their sell-by date. Changing circumstances offer a new option, an opportunity to develop trust in the infinite power of life which loves and sustains you, helping you to feel safe no matter what befalls you. They provide a chance to realise that actually, you are the director and producer of your life because it is your own choices, your most cherished dreams and your higher aspirations that ultimately determine your reality, your lifestyle and your experiences.

Change is an arcane magic. Magical change is what magicians do. That is how they transform the commonplace into the sensational. But magic is an invisible job. It is concealed in the depth of the experience. And likewise, the magic of change must start in the hidden privacy of your own mind, by changing your beliefs, your concepts and your thoughts. Start by accepting the fact that everything is possible. Yes, everything. All you need to do is to let go of limited thinking by constantly reminding yourself of your own divine identity as a child of God, trusting the unseen intelligence that guides your life and dwelling on your infinite, God-given creativity.

When you love yourself enough to realise that a good life is naturally yours, not something you have to earn or pay for, you are ready for a positive change. It is your birthright to aspire for the best and the finest you can imagine. It does, however, involve considerable soul-searching. You have to scrap old beliefs of limitations and adopt concepts of limitlessness. You have to dive deep within yourself to find out which false concepts are keeping you from accomplishing your heart's desires.

For example:

- Do you believe that life is fated so why risk a change?
- Do you believe that to succeed, you have to exert yourself relentlessly at work?
- Do you believe that to be successful you must be dishonest?
- Do you believe that money is the root of all evil?
- Do you doubt that you actually deserve to be happy?
- Do you doubt that prosperity is your natural birthright?
- Do you doubt that you already have what it takes to succeed?
- Do you think that life is not an experience to be enjoyed but a drudgery to be tolerated?

To assist the transition of thinking from one way to another, it helps to use counteracting affirmations, in which one undesired concept is reversed by an opposite one. These affirmations are best used to supplant negative thoughts as they creep in during mind chatter. You can make them yourself to suit your specific needs. Here, however, are a few examples:

- I choose to have faith, not fear.
- I am not powerless; I am one with the power of all creation.
- I now let go of limiting ideas and replace them with thoughts of my huge potential.
- I refuse to dwell on scarcity and instead claim my divine inheritance of abundance.
- I renounce thoughts of failure and adopt thoughts of success and prosperity.
- Living alone does not make my life loveless; I have all the love I need within my own heart.
- I release the past knowing that my future is not bounded by precedents.

One of the major impediments to change is our strong emotional attachment to things and people, and even more intensely, to opinions and beliefs. We live in a materialistic society in which we mentally attach great importance to our prized possessions. People are commonly more inclined to spend their lives pursuing their careers and amassing fortunes rather than pursuing their higher call for love, happiness and higher awareness. The thing is that our tight attachment to specific people or to physical entities such as property, valuables or money limits our thinking and deprives us of our inborn joy. Attachments are a recipe for frustration because they inhibit our growth and restrict our ability to flow with life's changes. This, however, does not mean that we should abandon our worldly goals. Having and enjoying material possessions is fine as long as we do not feel dependent upon them for our happiness or security. We must learn to detach a bit from being tightly connected emotionally to either cherished relationships or prized assets. And if ever, for any reason, we need to give up any of them, it makes it easier to remember that we actually do not own anything. In truth, what we have does not really belong to us. We only use it as custodians while we are here.

Practising non-attachment is long and gradual. At the start, it usually helps to pick one of the things to which you feel only slightly attached, and imagine for a day that you actually do not depend on it for your contentment. In your mind, start downgrading your addiction to this thing, to this person or to this situation, and reduce this addiction into a preference. When you think in terms of preference, it is no longer about things you must have but about things you prefer to have. Consequently, you release the need to control them. You thus come to enjoy a higher level of independence and happiness.

As far as relationships are concerned, do not equate attachment with love. Do not think that by lessening an attachment to a loved one you are becoming less sympathetic or less caring. You are actually raising your relationship to a higher level. You start relating to the good of your partner on a higher level, rather than to the inferior wants of their personality. As you allow them to make their mistakes, you reflect on any higher thing you can do for them, not necessarily on what they ask you to do on a lower level. As the popular saying goes, 'Give a man a fish and you feed him for the day; teach a man to fish and you feed him for life.' By practising a slight detachment, you gain a better perspective on how and when to offer care and assistance that will best serve your loved one's interests.

Our inner desires reflect the divine purpose. What you

deeply desire indicates what the universe wants you to have. The higher intelligence that gave you a particular desire will fulfil it through you if you are willing to believe in it without reservations. When you are fully determined to reach a goal, you will find it easier to open up to new changes that are necessary for its implementation. It is crucial, though, to stay tuned to your gut feelings and follow your inner urges to the letter. You have to learn to trust your inner guidance and go along with any new initiative you are being led to, even if it makes no logical sense.

A few years ago I read a story about a man who retired at the age of 50 in order to pursue a new career which he always dreamed about. He had previously spent 30 years in business, hating every minute of it, with only one purpose in mind: to save enough money so that he could afford to purchase a horse ranch and raise horses. At last he felt financially confident enough to quit his hateful job, buy a ranch and start doing what he always loved to do. To his great surprise, the horse ranch enterprise took off from day one. It prospered beyond his fondest dreams. In hindsight this man realised the futility of resisting change. Had he chosen to take the leap of faith and follow the strong urge to change the course of his life earlier, he could have saved himself many years of frustration.

Although you need to keep an open mind to new ideas and insights that come from within, it is useless to berate yourself for any unwise choices or decisions you once made, however stupid or faulty they may seem to you now, because you now see them from a higher perspective of awareness and with hindsight. Be willing to accept the past because your past is the foundation of your present, just as your present is a foundation of your future. All occurrences, no matter how you view them, are pieces in a huge jigsaw puzzle that makes up your life. Besides, we each grow at our own unique pace and to play the blame game can only serve to undermine our confidence and attract more similar undesirable events.

Life is constantly pushing us forward and upward to our higher good. There is no let up. Life is a constant chain of interconnected events and cycles, all perfectly sequenced. The problem is that most of us are creatures of habit to one degree or another. Once we have spent a period of time in a certain lifestyle, such as an occupation, a relationship or a domestic situation, we become set in our ways and tend to identify ourselves with these situations. Stale conditions, like dead-end jobs or dead-end relationships, actually propel us to seek better alternatives. Ultimately, these events lead us to expand our understanding and rise to higher levels of self-love, and eventually, to a higher level of existence. In a sense, all life events, whether we approve of them or not, are milestones in the path of spiritual evolution.

Once we have managed to grasp a well-needed lesson and rise to a certain level of awareness, we may be prompted by a new situation that presents a new challenge at a higher level. If similar problems and situations seem to occur again and again, you may realise that each time they come from a higher perspective. These new events can enable you to understand these situations better, or from a different angle. You may then be able to notice an erroneous behaviour pattern that needs to be rectified. Every experience contains purpose and meaning. By finding a way to look at the symbolic meaning of each experience, we can learn to face and adapt to the inevitable changes that life brings.

Times of change are times to take a chance with life. Changing circumstances not only herald new possibilities, they also offer a precious opportunity to take the leap of faith, overcome fear and show courage. It is time to remember the age-old saying: 'Fortune favours the brave.' Some people, however, feel safer by leaving things unchanged.

Yet, paradoxically, it is only by taking a risk that they can grow and expand and become more self-confident. People who shrink from taking risks eventually end up being more scared and insecure. Times of change impel us to adopt more optimistic views about life and urge us to believe in our growth and sense of direction. This means believing that the future holds a promise for the better and the higher. Embracing the new gets easier when you start realising that life is on your side and that any change, either imposed by external events or initiated by an inner urge, has been designed by your soul and is eventually always for your higher good.

Getting fed up with irritating situations or with a dull and cheerless lifestyle is one of the main catalysts for change. It creates a deep desire to rebel against frustrating conditions which hold you back. You must use this rebelling energy in a constructive way to forge ahead and propel yourself to the new and the better. Feelings of resentment and anger only make the change more difficult and painful. Likewise, if what you wish can come only if another person changes or acts differently, it is something you cannot control. You cannot impose your will on other people who resist change. You cannot force people to change, however beneficial it may be for them.

Variety is the spice of life. Without it, staleness and boredom that stifle the natural joie de vivre will prevail. 'They must often change who would be constant in happiness,' wrote Confucius, and Francis Bacon backed up this statement, saying, 'Nothing is pleasant that is not spiced by variety.'

Start with little daily changes. Try to do something differently every day. Change your daily routines. If you drive to work, try different routes. If you normally eat in the kitchen, try eating in the living room. From time to time, rearrange your furniture. Even more important, be open to consider new concepts and new attitudes of mind, once you suspect that the old ones do not seem right any more. If you always used to solve problems logically, try experimenting with lateral thinking. Try to view people and situations from different angles. Develop an inquisitive mind. Question everything. Take nothing for granted. Changing small bits in your life prepares you to accept bigger changes more readily. It helps dissolve the fear of the new.

By their nature, children adjust readily and spontaneously to changing situations. They happily embrace new experiences as exciting adventures and flow with them. But as we grow older, we tend to get set in our ways. Novel, fresh attitudes, however, revitalise sparkling energies of excitement and fulfilment. Opening up to new experiences boosts our sense of aliveness. It leads us to experience and live the present moment more intensely. Indeed, many people thrive on adventure. They seek this intense sense of liveliness by living on the edge. Mountain climbers, surfers, car racers and bungee jumpers know that they are taking a major risk. But they are consciously willing to risk their lives in exchange for experiencing the ultimate thrill of life to its full intensity. They need their adrenalin rush to feel alive.

Don't you think you deserve better than what you already have? It is your natural legacy as a child of God to be successful in everything you do. To doubt that means that you are doubting your divine identity. You are assuming a false inferior self. You are rejecting your birthright to prosper. You are depriving yourself of the highest and the finest. To claim your right you must seek new ways, new attitudes and new changes and be ready to embrace them when they arrive. Every time you embrace something new, you bring more aliveness into your life. You expand your capacity for joy. You extend your ability to have more. Life is constantly pushing us to grow through change. Eventually, it is the changes that we accept and embrace that assist us in rising to higher levels of fulfilment.

Every day is a new page in the story of your life. Every morning you wake up anew to fresh ideas and new possibilities. Think of the opportunities the day might bring instead of dwelling on past unhappy memories. If you must think of the past, deliberately focus only on those instances in which you were successful and happy. Do not dread the future. Do not think that the future will deprive you of anything valuable. Make the future your ally. Hold a picture in your mind that the future will be bright and better than anything you have ever known. Your mere expectation will draw it to you.

Epilogue

To my reader: I would like to express my deepest gratitude to you for joining me on this journey through the pages of this book. May something you read in one of these pages serve your higher good and help make a difference for the better in your life, as it did in mine.

To conclude, I would like to share with you the Principles for Desired Attitude, the Desiderata, which has been my guide for many years.

DESIDERATA

Go placidly amid the noise & haste, & remember what peace there may be in silence. As far as possible without surrender, be on good terms with all persons. Speak your truth quietly & clearly; and listen to others, even the dull & ignorant; they too have their story.

Avoid loud & aggressive persons, they are vexations to the spirit. If you compare yourself with others, you may become vain & bitter; for always there will be greater & lesser persons than yourself. Enjoy your achievements as well as your plans.

Keep interested in your own career, however humble; it is a real possession in the changing fortunes of time. Exercise caution in your business affairs; for the world is full of trickery. But let this not blind you to what virtue there is;

many persons strive for high ideals; and everywhere life is full of heroism.

Be yourself. Especially do not feign affection. Neither be cynical about love; for in the face of all aridity & disenchantment it is perennial as the grass.

Take kindly the counsel of the years, gracefully surrendering the things of youth. Nurture strength of spirit to shield you in sudden misfortune. But do not distress yourself with imaginings. Many fears are born of fatigue & loneliness. Beyond a wholesome discipline, be gentle with yourself.

You are a child of the universe, no less than the trees & the stars; you have a right to be here. And whether or not it is clear to you, no doubt the universe is unfolding as it should.

Therefore be in peace with God, whatever you conceive Him to be, and whatever your labours & aspirations, in the noisy confusion of life keep peace with your soul.

With all its sham, drudgery & broken dreams, it is still a beautiful world. Be careful. Strive to be happy.